THE NO-NONSENSE KEY

Read *Refinancing Your Mortgage* if

- You want to take advantage of newly-lowered interest rates
- You want to pay less each month on your mortgage
- You want to use your home equity to best advantage
- You want to make the most of one of your major financial assets

NO-NONSENSE FINANCIAL GUIDES:

How to Finance Your Child's College Education
How to Use Credit and Credit Cards
Understanding Treasury Bills and Other U.S. Government Securities
Understanding Tax-Exempt Bonds
Understanding Money Market Funds
Understanding Mutual Funds
Understanding IRAs
Understanding Common Stocks
Understanding the Stock Market
Understanding Stock Options and Futures Markets
How to Choose a Discount Stockbroker
How to Make Personal Financial Planning Work for You
How to Plan and Invest for Your Retirement
The New Tax Law and What It Means to You

NO-NONSENSE REAL ESTATE GUIDES:

Understanding Condominiums and Co-ops
Understanding Buying and Selling a House
Understanding Mortgages
Refinancing Your Mortgage

NO-NONSENSE LEGAL GUIDES:

Understanding Estate Planning and Wills
How to Choose a Lawyer

NO-NONSENSE REAL ESTATE GUIDE

REFINANCING YOUR MORTGAGE

Phyllis C. Kaufman
and Arnold Corrigan

LONGMEADOW PRESS

Refinancing Your Mortgage

Cover art © 1986 by Longmeadow Press. Design by Adrian Taylor. Production services by William S. Konecky Associates, New York.

ISBN: 0-681-40244-X

Printed in the United States of America

0 9 8 7 6 5 4 3 2

TABLE OF CONTENTS

PART 1   *Why Refinance?*

CHAPTER 1   Your Great Opportunity   5
CHAPTER 2   What Does Interest Cost?   7
CHAPTER 3   Your Mortgage and the Tax Reform
                Act of 1986   9

PART 2   *Your Mortgage—A Refresher Course*

CHAPTER 4   What Is A Mortgage and How Does It
                Work?   13
CHAPTER 5   Mortgage History Condensed and
                Simplified   15
CHAPTER 6   Types of Mortgages   18

PART 3   *The Decision to Refinance*

CHAPTER 7   The Costs of Refinancing   33
CHAPTER 8   The 3% Solution   39
CHAPTER 9   The Mathematics of Refinancing   41
CHAPTER 10   Points vs. Percentages   52

PART 4   *The Mechanics of Refinancing*

CHAPTER 11   Where to Refinance   57
CHAPTER 12   What Type of Mortgage Loan?   61
CHAPTER 13   Applying for Your New Mortgage   68
CHAPTER 14   Mortgage Insurance   71
CHAPTER 15   Special Situations—Refinancing
                Condominiums and Co-ops   73
CHAPTER 16   Ten Pitfalls and Their Cures   75
CHAPTER 17   Settlement—The Happy Ending   78

PART 5   *Alternatives to Refinancing*

CHAPTER 18   Second Mortgages and Home Equity
                Loans   83
Glossary   87
Appendices   93

To my friends
Peter and Bebe Benoliel

ACKNOWLEDGMENTS

The authors wish to express their gratitude to Harmon S. Spolan, Esquire, President of Jefferson Bank, Philadelphia, Pennsylvania, for generously sharing with us his knowledge and expertise. We are also grateful to the staff of Jefferson Bank for their kind assistance and support.

PART 1
WHY REFINANCE?

1
YOUR GREAT OPPORTUNITY

Owning a home is the American dream. But in recent years, paying for a home has become the American nightmare.

One reason for the nightmare is that housing prices have risen. But an even bigger reason has been the rise in mortgage costs. The average interest rate on a home mortgage climbed from less than 6% in 1965 to around 9% by 1975, and then to an astounding peak of over 15% in 1981. For the whole period from 1980 to 1985, mortgage rates averaged about 13%.

But the millions of homeowners who took on mortgages at high rates between 1979 and 1985 now have another chance. By early 1986, for the first time in many years, mortgages were being offered in some cities at "single-digit" levels—that is, below 10%.

If you are planning to buy a home, the drop in interest rates represents a great opportunity. But if you already have a mortgage taken when rates were high, you have perhaps an even greater opportunity. You can replace your present mortgage with a new lower-rate mortgage, saving money every month and possibly obtaining other benefits as well.

That's what this book is about. It will tell you how to "refinance" your mortgage in the best possible way, and in a way that meets your individual needs. We think this book will also be of great help to those who are taking out a mortgage for the first time.

Was it a mistake to take out a mortgage when rates were high? Of course not. If you wanted to buy a home between 1979 and 1985, you had little choice. Home ownership has, we hope, given you pleasure, comfort, and security. Your home has probably appreciated in value and you have enjoyed considerable tax benefits. Paying off a mortgage regularly has boosted your credit rating and qualified you as a more financially responsible individual.

Advantages of Refinancing

What will you accomplish by refinancing? If you take out a new lower-rate mortgage loan for the amount of the remaining principal balance on your old mortgage, and running for the same number of years, you accomplish one very simple, important goal: you reduce the size of your monthly mortgage payment. Home ownership will give you the same benefits as before, but it will cost you substantially less money.

If the monthly payments are still burdensome, you may in some cases be able to reduce them still further by stretching out the term of your loan—that is, the number of years over which you will have to make payments. For example, if you originally obtained a 20-year, $50,000 mortgage in 1980, you could now probably refinance for 30 years, stretching out your payments over a longer period.

Or you may decide to go in the opposite direction, keeping your monthly payments around their present level, but paying off your loan in a shorter period of years.

Refinancing Your Mortgage gives you the inside track on refinancing—the how's, when's, why's, and the pitfalls that could cost you time and money.

2
WHAT DOES INTEREST COST?

The interest you pay on your mortgage loan costs a staggering amount of money over the years. If you are paying 13% or 14% interest on a 30-year mortgage, your payments of principal and interest will eventually total approximately four times the original amount of your mortgage.

Consider a 13%, 30-year mortgage loan of $40,000. Before you can call your home truly yours, you will pay $119,289 in interest in addition to repaying the $40,000 face value of the loan, making your total payments $159,289. If you have the same terms, but a $100,000 loan, you will pay $298,228 of interest, and your total payments will be $398,228.

The following table shows how much *interest* you will pay on different size mortgages at varying interest rates. Note that the dollar amounts shown *do not include the principal amount* of your mortgage (in this case, $40,000, $70,000, or $100,000), which must of course also be repaid.

It's obvious from the table that refinancing your mortgage at a lower interest rate can save you large amounts of money. But there are costs of refinancing to consider. And since a mortgage deal is always one of the biggest and most important arrangements in your financial life, you want to arrange a mortgage that is as closely tailored as possible to your individual needs. Before we calculate your specific savings from refinancing (see Chapter 9), let's look at some of the general tax and financial considerations you should keep in mind while doing your mortgage planning.

Total Interest Payments on a Mortgage

Mortgage Term & Amount	Interest Rate								
	7%	8%	9%	10%	11%	12%	13%	14%	15%
15 Years									
$ 40,000	$ 24,716	$ 28,808	$ 33,026	$ 37,371	$ 41,833	$ 46,411	$ 51,096	$ 55,885	$ 60,769
70,000	43,252	50,413	57,796	65,400	73,210	81,220	89,419	97,798	106,348
100,000	61,789	72,019	82,567	93,428	104,586	116,029	127,743	139,713	151,924
30 Years									
$ 40,000	55,804	65,662	75,862	86,367	97,131	108,118	119,289	130,622	142,077
70,000	97,656	114,909	132,763	151,148	169,983	189,207	208,759	228,588	248,640
100,000	139,512	164,157	189,663	215,925	242,835	270,300	298,228	326,553	355,198

3
YOUR MORTGAGE AND THE TAX REFORM ACT OF 1986

One of the major changes made by the Tax Reform Act of 1986 is the treatment of deductions for interest payments. While the deduction for many types of interest payments is being phased out, interest on a home mortgage is still generally deductible. But there are limits.

First, the deduction for "qualified residence interest" under the 1986 law *is limited to interest on debt taken against a taxpayer's principal residence or second residence only.*

Second, with the exceptions noted below, *the debt on which interest is deductible may not exceed the cost basis of the property*—the original purchase price plus the cost of any improvements.

Your Cost Basis

Since your cost basis takes on this added importance, you must keep careful track of the amount spent on improvements. If you bought your home for $80,000 and have since spent $4,000 for a finished basement and $8,000 for a new kitchen, your new cost basis will be $92,000, and you can deduct interest paid on a mortgage loan of up to $92,000.

In addition, if you paid any state or local tax on the purchase of your home, that tax can be included as part of your cost basis under the new law.

(Note: *if you refinanced your mortgage or took out a new mortgage before August 17, 1986,* the mortgage can be up to the *fair market value of the property,* and the interest will still be fully deductible, even if the fair market value exceeds the cost basis.)

The Educational-Medical Exception

There is another intriguing exception to the cost basis rule: the debt can exceed your cost basis to the extent it is incurred for educational or medical expenses, and the interest will still be deductible. (The educational expenses may include reasonable living expenses for students away from home.)

What is a Residence?

Note that the tax law specifically defines "residence" for the purpose of the mortgage deduction. Specifically, if one of your homes, such as a vacation home, is rented out part of the time, mortgage interest will be fully deductible as "qualified residence interest" only if you use the home personally for the *greater* of (a) 14 days or (b) 10% of the number of days for which the home is rented out. Otherwise, the mortgage interest will be considered as an expense of the rental activity, and it will be deductible only against the rental income, or against other rental or similar income.

And the debt must be on a *residence*. If you own land on which you hope someday to build a vacation home, any interest you pay on a loan against that land will not be deductible as long as no residence has yet been built on the land.

Borrowing For More Than Your Cost Basis

Should you ever borrow for more than your tax basis, so that part of the mortgage interest you pay will not be tax-deductible? Yes—if you need to borrow a substantial amount, borrowing on your home may be the only practical way to do it. Also, whatever the size of the borrowing, interest rates secured by your home are generally considerably lower than other consumer interest rates—and note that the tax deduction on other forms of consumer interest is being phased out under the 1986 law. (For more information, see the No-Nonsense Financial Guide, *The New Tax Law and What It Means To You*.)

But whether the interest is deductible or not, beware of borrowing unwisely. You will have to repay the money you borrow, with interest. *And your home is pledged as security for the loan*. Don't take this extra risk without very good reason.

PART 2
YOUR MORTGAGE: A REFRESHER COURSE

4
WHAT IS A MORTGAGE AND HOW DOES IT WORK?

We tend to use the word *mortgage* for convenience, while we really are talking about a *mortgage loan*. When we speak about "getting a mortgage," we actually mean obtaining a *mortgage loan*. The mortgage itself is not a loan, but a *pledge*.

To make sure that you understand how both your old mortgage and your new mortgage work, we offer a brief refresher course.

Let's look at how a mortgage works. A bank or other lender gives you the money needed for the purchase of your home or, later, simply as a loan based upon the value of your home. In return, you give the lender a mortgage (pledge); you pledge your property as security for repayment of the loan. In addition, you promise to pay interest at an agreed-on rate or according to an agreed-on formula.

The Lien on Your Property

Your lender registers your pledge with the appropriate local authority. The registration is called a *lien*. A lien is a legal notice that if the property is sold or if you fail to repay on schedule, the lien holder (your mortgage lender) has a legal means, called foreclosure, of taking possession of the property in order to be repaid. The lien becomes a first right against the property, taking precedence over almost all other obligations, except the tax collector. After you pay off your mortgage loan, plus the interest, the lien is removed and the pledged property is yours free and clear.

When you settled (closed) on your home, your mortgage lender gave you a check for the face amount of the mortgage

13

loan and you handed it over for payment to the seller together with your down payment.

Your name was recorded on the deed as the holder of title to the property, and your mortgage lender recorded its lien with the appropriate local authority.

Note: in some states, a Deed of Trust is used instead of a mortgage. A Deed of Trust fulfills the same purpose but works differently: the borrower deeds the property to a trustee as pledge for repayment.

When you refinance, your new mortgage lender will give you a check for the face value of your new mortgage. With this check you will pay off your existing mortgage. The lien of the old mortgage lender will be removed from your deed and your new mortgage lender will formally file his/her lien against your property.

5
MORTGAGE HISTORY CONDENSED AND SIMPLIFIED

Before we discuss the details of refinancing, let's take a moment to review a bit of mortgage history so that you will understand how we got to where we are and why refinancing can now be of such great value to so many people.

Until the late 1970's, mortgages generally were fixed-rate instruments that matured in anywhere from 15 to 30 years. Your interest rate was fixed at the very beginning, and you paid the same amount each and every month for the life of the loan.

Soaring Interest Rates

Then, in the 1970's, interest rates in general began to soar and mortgage interest rates went through the ceiling. By 1980-81, mortgage interest rates of 15%, 17%, and even 18% were commonplace.

The banks and other lenders who were holding old mortgages at rates of 5% to 7% suffered because they were collecting money at low interest rates on old mortgages while they had to borrow money at the new higher rates in order to conduct their business. The problem was enormous. Some lenders went bankrupt, many went out of business, and the financial industry realized that a change had to be made in mortgage lending. And change it did, in two critical ways.

Adjustable Rate Mortgages

First, the industry introduced the *adjustable rate mortgage* or ARM. In an ARM, the mortgage interest rate adjusts periodically

15

according to some general index of interest rates, so that the interest rate risk is shifted from the lender to the borrower. If interest rates rise, the lender is largely protected. (See Chapter 6.)

ARMs quickly began to represent roughly half the new mortgages issued. And with the ARM came a dazzling range of variations, advertised as being tailored to meet the needs of the borrower (though often of advantage mainly to the lender), such as Graduated Payment Mortgages, Elastic Mortgages, Balloon Mortgages, etc. (These will be reviewed in Chapter 6.)

The Secondary Mortgage Market

At the same time, it became apparent that the traditional mortgage lenders—savings and loans, commercial banks, savings banks—had neither the lending nor risk-taking capacity to satisfy the needs of the fast-expanding mortgage market. As a result, there was a virtual explosion in the *secondary market*, that is, the market in which mortgages are sold by the original lender to other investors. This arrangement has the advantage of bringing new capital into the market and freeing the lender's funds so that the lender once again has the capacity to originate new mortgages.

Financial institutions began to develop new ways of putting together packages of mortgages to sell to investors. Ways were found of assuring these investors that their investments were safe. With this assurance, the secondary market grew at a remarkable rate.

Fannie, Ginnie, and Freddie

Three government agencies—nicknamed Fannie Mae, Ginnie Mae, and Freddie Mac—have played an important part in the growth of secondary mortgage markets.

Fannie Mae

The Federal National Mortgage Association, known as Fannie Mae (FNMA), was chartered by the government in 1938. It raises capital by borrowing from the public through the sale of mortgage-backed bonds, and uses the money to buy mortgages from mortgage lenders, giving the lenders cash to begin the cycle over again. In 1970, while retaining some of the privileges of a governmental agency, Fannie Mae became a private business, owned by participating lenders and the public.

Ginnie and Freddie

The Government National Mortgage Association (Ginnie Mae) (GNMA) is actually part of the Department of Housing and Urban Development (HUD). It buys certain mortgages, packages them into pools, and sells participations in these pools to investors, who receive monthly payments representing both principal and interest. These participations, termed *pass-through certificates,* carry the "full faith and credit" of the U.S.Government—the best of all guarantees—and have become immensely popular with investors as a result.

The Federal Home Loan Mortgage Corporation (Freddie Mac), the third and last of the trio, is part of the Federal Home Loan Bank Board, which oversees savings and loan associations. It buys certain mortgages, raising capital by selling mortgage-backed bonds to the public, like Fannie Mae.

Fannie and Freddie and Refinancing

Fannie Mae and Freddie Mac are important forces in the refinancing business as well. When a lender approves a loan for refinancing, the lender most likely will look to resell the new mortgage commitment. Both Fannie Mae and Freddie Mac have established guidelines regarding the types of mortgages they will purchase. These guidelines apply to refinancing and, if your needs fit within their parameters, it may be easier for you to refinance at the most favorable terms. (See Chapter 11.)

6
TYPES OF MORTGAGES

Today's Market

The decline in interest rates has brought a swing away from the adjustable rate mortgage (ARM) and the many new variations that came with it. In 1985 and 1986, as interest rates dropped to levels not seen since the 1970's, the majority of borrowers have opted for fixed-rate mortgages, and the lenders have generally been willing to oblige them. With a fixed-rate mortgage, as pointed out earlier, your interest rate and your monthly payments are fixed for the life of the loan.

Analyze Your Mortgage

Before you begin to consider refinancing, you must understand your existing mortgage. No doubt you have a copy of your mortgage loan contract, though it may be hidden away in a file or safe deposit box. This is the time to take it out and read it, cover to cover, fine print included. You need to be sure exactly how your interest rate is determined, and you need to know what penalty, if any, you incur if you pay off your mortgage early in order to refinance.

If you have trouble understanding the terms and conditions, don't hesitate to ask your lender questions. You might seek expert assistance if you need an interpretation (which may well be the case). Your attorney can help you, or the attorney who handled your closing (settlement).

Obviously, you need to understand how your present interest rate works in order to understand if refinancing is worthwhile. Also, understanding your present contract may give you good hints as to what to avoid or include in your refinancing agreement.

Remember that you have a right to clarification by your lender. If you have an ARM from a nationally chartered bank, they were legally obligated to give you information on how your ARM would work if interest rates went up by 2% over 5 years. They also had to tell you which index was being used in determining your actual interest rate. But apart from this specific legal obligation, any reputable lender should give you a complete explanation of your mortgage at the time of inception and should be willing to provide any information you may need later on.

Prepayment Penalty

The first thing to check is whether your mortgage contract contains a prepayment penalty, that is, a penalty for paying off the mortgage early, before the stated maturity date. If there is a penalty, it may be sizable—sometimes as much as 6 months' interest. Many states prohibit these penalties, but others do not. So whether your mortgage carries such a penalty is likely to depend more on the state where you live than on your individual lender.

Conventional Mortgages

Mortgages can be classified in several ways. Before going on to discuss other aspects of mortgages, it will be useful to make the important distinction between conventional mortgages and federally sponsored mortgages.

A conventional mortgage is any type of mortgage loan that is not insured by an agency of the federal government. Conventional mortgages can be either the standard fixed-rate loan or any one of the adjustable-rate varieties.

The majority of mortgages are "conventional." Remember that it is not the actual terms of the loan, the number of years it will run, or the interest rate, that makes it conventional—it is simply that the loan does not carry government insurance. As a result, the prevailing interest rate on conventional mortgages is generally higher than on government-insured mortgages.

The fact that your conventional mortgage may be resold to Fannie Mae, Freddie Mac, or Ginnie Mae (see Chapter 5) does not change the basic character of your loan. If it is made conventionally, it remains a conventional mortgage throughout its life.

Assumability

Having made the distinction, we can now point out that federally sponsored mortgages are *assumable,* while many (though not all) conventional mortgages are not. An assumable mortgage is one that can be taken over by the buyer, when you decide to sell your home; the buyer can assume your old mortgage at your interest rate. If your interest rate is lower than the prevailing rate at the time of resale, this feature could add an extra value to your house and make it more salable. Obviously, when refinancing, you should try to make your new mortgage assumable if you can.

Federally Sponsored Mortgages

Federally-backed mortgages include loans that are secured by the Federal Housing Authority (FHA), the Veterans Administration (VA), and the Farmers Home Administration (FmHA).

FHA

The purpose of the Federal Housing Authority (FHA), a part of the U.S. Department of Housing and Urban Development (HUD), is to encourage home ownership by those who, without the assistance of the federal government, would not be able to afford to buy their own home.

The Federal Housing Authority (FHA) does not actually lend mortgage money. Rather, it offers loan insurance programs that can assist in obtaining 30-year mortgage loans with a small downpayment. These programs insure your mortgage against default, and the insurance makes the mortgage attractive to a lender despite the small downpayment.

There are no special economic qualifications for borrowers to receive FHA insurance. But the property, which may be urban or rural, new or existing, must meet the HUD Minimum Property Standards. And there is a maximum dollar limit above which the FHA will not insure.

All FHA loans are assumable and refinanceable without penalty.

Veterans Administration

The Veterans Administration (VA) guarantees that eligible veterans will be able to get mortgages with *no money down*. If the veteran defaults, the VA will pay off the mortgage loan. Like FHA loans, VA loans are assumable and can be refinanced without penalty.

FmHA

Farmers Home Administration Loans (FmHA) are available to farmers and to non-farmers who live within specified rural areas and who meet certain low-income requirements. The FmHA is part of the U.S. Department of Agriculture.

Mortgage Terms—Fixed-Rate Mortgages

A fixed-rate mortgage is the standard, old-reliable mortgage that your parents had and that, until mortgage interest rates began to soar, was usually the only kind of mortgage available. And it will probably be the type of mortgage you choose when you refinance.

In a fixed-rate mortgage, as we have said, the interest rate is determined at the time the loan is arranged and remains constant through the life of the loan. You always know how much your monthly payments will be, because they never vary from the first to the last installment.

The consistency and security of knowing exactly how much your payments will be is certainly an advantage of the fixed-rate loan. And if you start out with an interest rate that you consider favorable, it is comforting to know that your payments will not be subject to the fluctuations and vagaries of the interest rate market.

Adjustable Rate Mortgage (ARM)

The basic Adjustable Rate Mortgage (ARM) is usually called an Adjustable Mortgage Loan (AML) at federal savings and loan associations, and is also referred to as a Variable Rate Mortgage. For convenience and brevity, we will refer to all of these as ARMs.

An ARM is a mortgage where the interest rate is adjusted at fixed intervals during the life of the loan according to a specific index. This index is some accepted indicator of interest rates—for example, the current 90-day Treasury Bill rate (the interest rate the U.S. Treasury pays on its shortest-term borrowings), or the rate on longer-term Treasury borrowings, or sometimes an index of actual prevailing mortgage rates. So the interest rate you pay on your mortgage loan changes periodically (every 6 months or every 1, 3, or 5 years) based on fluctuations in the general level of interest rates.

As we have said, ARMs came into fashion when interest rates were soaring and have become less popular now that interest rates have declined. But you may still be offered an ARM as a refinancing option; and if your existing mortgage is an ARM, you need to understand the terms in order to consider intelligently whether refinancing is worthwhile.

We noted above that the interest rate you pay on an ARM is generally based on some interest rate index. But a critical factor is the "margin," the percentage that is added to the index to arrive at the interest rate you actually pay. The margin will vary depending on the index used and your particular loan arrangement. The margin may, for example, be 2½% or 3% if your lender is using a Treasury Bill index (since Treasury Bill rates are among the lowest interest rates in the market), but it should be small or zero if you are using a national mortgage index.

Let's take an example: assume your initial interest rate was 12%. After 3 years, the time for your first rate adjustment has come, and Treasury Bills (your index) are now paying 9½%. Sounds great? Not really. Your lender built in a margin of 3%, so your rate goes up to 12½% (9½% plus 3%). And your monthly payments are adjusted upward accordingly.

Caps

Most ARMs include a "cap" provision, to protect the borrower against unlimited skyrocketing of payments if interest rates rise.

22

There are two kinds of caps—a life cap and an adjustment cap. A life cap puts a maximum on the amount that your interest rate or monthly payments can be raised over the entire life of the loan. An adjustment cap puts a maximum on the amount of each individual adjustment. The best ARM, when interest rates were soaring, was one that had both kinds of caps. A favorable mortgage, for example, might have limited interest rate increases to a maximum of ½% at each adjustment period and a total of 5% over the life of the loan.

Just as an ARM may have put an upper cap on interest rates, however, there may have been a minimum cap, too. A minimum cap could be preventing you from enjoying the advantages of lower interest rates now, and might be one good reason to refinance. Check your ARM to see how low your payments can drop as interest rates decline.

There's another important distinction where caps are concerned. The cap may be on the *interest rate* you pay or on the *dollar amount* you pay each month. An interest rate cap is simple and straightforward enough. But a dollar amount cap can be treacherous. When interest rates rise, a dollar amount cap will limit the rise in your monthly payments, but the mortgage terms will often call for you to be charged eventually for any amount by which your monthly payments fall short of the current effective interest rate. You then fall prey to what is termed *negative amortization.*

Negative Amortization

Negative amortization has become uncommon recently, but it has presented many troublesome problems to mortgage borrowers in the past. If your current mortgage includes a potential for negative amortization, that alone may be a strong argument in favor of refinancing.

Let us explain. *Amortization* is the process by which you gradually pay off the principal amount of your mortgage loan. *Negative amortization* is what happens when the process goes into reverse. If your monthly payments are "capped" at a level where you are not paying the effective interest charges on your mortgage, the lender may have the right to add the difference to the principal of your loan. So, while you are making bargain monthly payments, you are actually accumulating more and more debt.

Here's a specific example. It was not uncommon, during the period of high interest rates, for mortgage lenders to offer special "bargain" initial interest rates to borrowers. These rates were usually not tied to the index. Moreover, in some cases the borrower was charged for the difference between the "bargain" initial-year rate and the rate as calculated from the index. Let's say that you paid a 9⅞% initial interest rate for the first year. And let's assume that for the first year and for all subsequent years, the index called for an interest rate of 12½%. (A non-fluctuating index rate is unlikely, but we use it here to simplify our example.) Let's also assume a dollar cap on payments—when your payments were adjusted each year, the maximum increase could only be 7½% of the dollar amount each year, no matter how high the interest rate index was.

The table below shows how this worked. For the first four years, while you were enjoying your "bargain" payments, your loan was actually *increasing* in size. Later on, of course, you had to pay more to make up for this. Such arrangements were not uncommon—you may be one of those whose mortgage balance is still higher than the original loan amount.

Amount of Loan	Index Percent	Year Number	Monthly Payments	Loan Balance
$70,000	9⅞%	1	$607.84	$71,542.30
	12½%	2	653.43	72,709.29
		3	702.44	73,407.78
		4	755.12	73,529.11
		5	811.75	72,946.64
		6–30	795.38	

Negative Amortization and Total Caps

Many mortgage loans contained a total cap on negative amortization, often 125% of the original mortgage balance, so that if your original loan was $100,000, the lender could only negatively amortize up to a loan balance of $125,000. If that happened, however, the burden was probably on you rather than on the lender; you were probably required to come up with a lump-sum payment or some refinancing arrangement to keep the loan balance from rising above the limit.

So negative amortization was definitely an ARM concern. However, we repeat that if *your mortgage had a cap on interest rates, rather than on dollar payments, there could be no negative amortization.*

Balloon Mortgage

Balloon mortgages were very common in the early 1980's. With a balloon mortgage, the loan behaves initially like a regular fixed-rate mortgage. You make payments at first at the same rate as if the debt were scheduled to last for a long period, usually 30 years. However, you actually make these payments only for a specific shorter period, often 3 or 5 years, or perhaps 10. At the conclusion of that period, the entire remaining principal amount becomes due.

Here's an example: Let's assume you took out a 30-year mortgage for $40,000 at 12½% with a three-year balloon. Each month for 35 months (just short of the 3 years), you paid $426.90. In the 36th month, however, you would have to pay the mortgage lender $39,982.68, the total balance due on your loan. The payments you made in the first years of your mortgage went largely, as usual, to pay the interest owed, with little being applied to repay principal. This is why your balance remained so high.

Balloon mortgages require refinancing at balloon time. If you have such a mortgage, due now or in the next few years, this could be the ideal time to refinance and eliminate both your balloon and your (probably) high interest rate.

Elastic Mortgage

An elastic mortgage combines the stability of fixed monthly payments with the flexibility of an ARM.

How does it do this? An elastic mortgage begins as a 15-year mortgage, with monthly payments fixed, permanently and absolutely, as of the date the mortgage is granted. If you pay $850 the first month, you will pay $850 each and every month thereafter. But unlike a fixed-rate loan, the interest rate can and does change according to a standard index (usually long-term Treasury Bonds).

This change in the interest rate is not reflected in the amount of your monthly payments; as stated above, they remain constant. It is reflected in the *number of payments* you make. If the interest rate index declines, your monthly payments may end before the end of the originally contracted 15 years. But if the interest rate index rises, you may have to make more payments, stretching beyond the original 15 years. So it is the term that varies instead of the monthly payment amount.

Interest rates on elastic mortgages were usually pegged initially about 2% below rates on regular fixed-rate instruments, since the borrower was taking a large part of the interest rate risk away from the lender. If you are now paying off such a mortgage, you may be in a fortunate position, and you will have to calculate carefully to see if refinancing really will be cost-effective for you before you decide to proceed.

Fixed-Rate Mortgage with a Call Option

These mortgages operate like an ordinary fixed-rate instrument, except that they have an additional provision which can make them operate like a balloon mortgage. Upon the occurrence of a predetermined condition, the lender has the right to "call" the loan. This means that the lender can demand immediate payment of the entire outstanding sum of the loan and you will have to refinance. This could come at a time when interest rates are high.

If you have a fixed-rate mortgage with a call option, we definitely recommend refinancing to eliminate the uncertainty of this lender privilege.

Graduated Payment Mortgage (GPM)

The graduated payment mortgage (GPM) was one of the more popular mortgage variations, designed to assist people—especially young people just getting started—who couldn't afford large monthly payments, but who had the potential to do so in the future. GPMs were either fixed-rate or adjustable rate. They were frequently called "yuppie" mortgage loans because of their attraction for young, upwardly mobile professionals.

The GPM theory was a good one, if you fit into the category described. You made smaller payments at the beginning of the loan, with your payments rising on a fixed schedule over the first years of the mortgage (usually 5, sometimes 10).

As an example of a graduated payment mortgage, let's assume that you got a $40,000 GPM at 12½% for 30 years. The payments that you made for the first years (in our example, 5 years) did not reflect the 12½% interest rate. Rather, they were precalculated based on an escalating scale under which you did not begin to amortize your loan (that is, begin to pay off the principal) until the 6th year. The payments escalated based on a fixed percentage; in our example, the dollar payments were raised by 7½% per year.

Under this example, you paid $329.43 per month for the first 12 months. Because the amount paid did not reflect the *real* interest rate of 12½%, a certain negative amortization was built into the calculations. But in this case the negative amortization was intentional, and you knew exactly how it accumulated. There were no surprises.

Let's look at a table:

Year Number	Monthly Payment	Loan Balance
1	$329.43	$41,108.95
2	354.14	42,050.63
3	380.70	42,770.38
4	409.25	43,241.69
5	439.94	43,375.08
6–30	472.94	

You will note that the loan balance went up in years 1 through 5, reflecting negative amortization. If this had been a $40,000 fixed rate mortgage at 12½% for 30 years, your monthly payments would have been a constant $426.90. Instead, the payments in our example rise every year, reaching a fixed level of $472.94 beginning in year 6. So the monthly payments in our example end up being $46.04 more each month than under a fixed mortgage; this was the price you paid for the privilege of paying less in the beginning. Such a deal could have been useful, if you were short of cash at first but were sure of being able to afford the later payments.

If you are still paying off a GPM and are still at the stage of negative amortization, refinancing will almost certainly make sense. If your payments have reached the stable stage, you should analyze your GPM like any fixed-rate mortgage and make your refinancing decision based on the merits discussed in Chapters 7 to 9.

Growing Equity Mortgage (GEM)

The growing equity mortgage had a twist that made your equity in the house increase faster. You paid a bit more each year, and that extra amount made for faster repayment of the debt principal. The increase in your payments was based on a predetermined percentage, typically 7½% each year. The schedule called for your debt to be paid off in considerably less than the usual 30 years, usually in 15 to 17 years.

When you refinance this type of mortgage, you will be able to do so for considerably less than with an ordinary fixed rate instrument because of your early accumulation of equity. In addition, your GEM will probably allow you to refinance for additional cash because of your increased equity.

Price Level Adjustable Mortgage

A price level adjustable mortgage is a type of ARM in which your interest payments theoretically remain constant in terms of real buying power. Monthly payments were adjusted according to an inflation index such as the consumer price index, with the added cost of inflation tacked on to the principal of the loan. So your interest rate didn't change, but your principal balance changed.

A mortgage borrower with this type of loan can greatly benefit from the stability of fixed-rate refinancing.

Rollover Mortgage

Also known as a renegotiable rate mortgage, this was really a long-term mortgage loan on which the interest rate was renegotiated either up or down at prearranged intervals of usually 3 to 5 years. As with an ARM, the maximum that the interest rate could be raised is predetermined.

These loans should be treated, for refinancing purposes, just like ARMs.

(For additional information on the various types of mortgages, see The No-Nonsense Real Estate Guide, *Understanding Mortgages.*)

PART 3
THE DECISION TO REFINANCE

7
THE COSTS OF REFINANCING

Unfortunately, it costs money to save money by refinancing. And, depending on your particular situation, the costs of refinancing can be steep, sometimes running as high as $5,000 or more. It is for this reason that refinancing, while decreasing your monthly payments, is not cost-effective in all cases.

Refinancing may sound like a simple exchange of your existing mortgage for a new mortgage carrying a lower interest rate. But in practice it isn't that simple. The mortgage lenders can't prevent you from prepaying your mortgage and getting out from under that old, high interest rate, but they can and do find ways to make some money out of the refinancing process.

Credit Check

When you want to refinance, the mortgage lender, whether it is your original lender or a new lender, will make a new judgment of your repayment potential. Are you a good credit risk? Have you made your mortgage payments regularly so that it is reasonable to assume that you will continue to do so in the future? You will probably have to pay $25 to $50 for your new lender to do a credit check to determine your credit history.

Another Settlement

When you refinance, you will have to go through a process very much like the original settlement on your home. You may remember the various charges, usually called "points," that you, as the mortgage borrower, had to pay. Well, points are about to enter your life again.

Points

Points are charges that the mortgage lender may require you to pay at settlement. Each point represents a one-time charge of 1% of the total amount of the mortgage loan. Points can be assessed by your mortgage lender to cover specific cost items, but they are often simply a way for the lender to make more money without raising the stated interest rate. Origination fees, placement fees, participation fees, and commitment fees all are names for non-specific charges that are likely to cost you cash at settlement; each is most frequently expressed in points.

It is not uncommon for a mortgage lender to charge 3 points for refinancing. If you are refinancing for $50,000, each point is equivalent to $500, and 3 points will cost $1,500. If you are refinancing for $100,000, a point equals $1,000 and 3 points equal $3,000, and so on.

Obviously, the less points charged, the lower your refinancing cost. It's worth shopping around among various mortgage lenders to find the best deal with the fewest points and lowest refinancing charges.

Deductibility of Points

How points paid for refinancing can be deducted on your income tax return is a complex question. When you buy a new home, you can usually take an immediate tax deduction for points paid on your mortgage, as if the points represented an immediate payment of interest. But in refinancing, the rules are less favorable.

As of the writing of this book, the general rule is that points may be deducted only by spreading the deduction over the life of the mortgage loan, but an immediate deduction is permitted if the points were paid in connection with the purchase of your principal residence. The immediate deduction doesn't apply to refinancing because you already own the property. An immediate deduction is also permitted if points are paid for the purpose of securing money to be used for improvement of your principal residence. In this case, payment of points must be standard practice in your area and the number of points you pay must not be excessive, in order for you to qualify for an immediate deduction. As these rules are complicated, we suggest that you consult your tax attorney or accountant.

Prepayment Penalty

As mentioned earlier, all mortgage loan contracts permit prepayment of part or all of the outstanding balance, but some do so only with a penalty. You must check your mortgage carefully to see if a penalty applies in your case. If it does, you may be required to pay as much as six months' extra interest to pay off your existing mortgage loan. This is a big bite and will definitely affect your refinancing equation.

Buy-Down

Although buy-downs are rare now that interest rates have declined, you should be aware of what a buy-down is and how it works.

In a buy-down arrangement, a mortgage borrower might pay the lender the cash equivalent of one or several points of interest so that the buyer then has a lower interest rate to pay on the mortgage loan. In a permanent buy-down, the borrower pays the cash equivalent of interest points for the life of the loan.

A more prevalent type of buy-down is not relevant to the refinancing situation. That type is the temporary buy-down, where the seller or builder of a house, who wants to encourage a buyer to purchase, makes a payment to reduce the interest rate on the mortgage for a limited number of years. A common arrangement is to buy down the rate by 3% in the first year of the mortgage, 2% in the second, and 1% in the third.

Title Insurance

Title to a property signifies possession of that property and conveys with it absolute control and ownership over the land and everything that is on the land, including houses, trees, air, etc. The *deed* is the written representation of title.

A marketable title is one that is reasonably free from

defects and that conveys the right to use, sell, and enjoy the property without unreasonable restrictions on the purchaser. All sorts of defects may exist in titles. In most states, a title company searches the title to the property and gives a full title report. In other states, the title search, called an Abstract of Title or an Attorney's Record Search, is done by a specialized attorney and followed by an attorney's opinion as to the condition of the title.

The result of the title abstract or search is contained in the opinion or report which is presented at settlement. Despite this report, it is essential for the buyer of any property to purchase title insurance. This is readily available and it insures that the title is good, clear, and marketable, and that if any title problems arise, the title insurer will pay to have them cleared.

When you refinance your mortgage, you will have to purchase additional title insurance, to assure your mortgage lender that you own good, clear, and marketable title to your property. This should present no problem, assuming that you purchased title insurance when you purchased your present home and that any problems were dealt with at that time.

Title Insurance Bring-Down

Reissuing the title insurance is usually less costly than issuing new insurance. The typical cost for title insurance for refinancing is $1,000. However, if you purchased your home within three years of refinancing, your new mortgage lender should allow you to "bring down" your existing title insurance and pay only a new fee equal to the prorated cost of the insurance. So if you refinance within three years of your initial purchase, your title insurance cost should not exceed $500.

Appraisal

Your new mortgage lender will require you to pay for a new appraisal of your property. Obviously, because your home is the security for the mortgage loan, its market value must be greater than the amount of the mortgage you request. The appraisal should cost approximately $250. If your property has appreciated in value, you may have the option of refinancing for more than the amount of your old mortgage balance. (See Chapter 3.)

Termite Inspection

Many jurisdictions and many lenders require a termite inspection and report on your home as part of the mortgage process. This usually costs about $100.

Miscellaneous

There are several miscellaneous charges and fees that you may have to pay to refinance. These include filing fees, document preparation fees, etc. These fees should not total more than $250 in most areas. If you think your mortgage lender is overcharging, you should shop a few other lenders, inquiring about their fee structure. Many fees are the result of state law or local ordinance and will be uniform within a given jurisdiction.

Be aware also that approximately 14 states charge a mortgage registration tax, based on the size of the mortgage loan; and some will require a new site survey to be done. The survey should cost between $250 and $350.

Professional Fees

You may want to engage the services of an attorney and/or accountant to help you analyze your current mortgage, assess the economic benefits of refinancing, and attend settlement. Make sure that you ask any professional to give you an estimate of his/her fee structure before beginning work.

Prepaid Items

Most states and localities require that certain items be prepaid for a given number of years at settlement. These items, which often total about $1,500, usually include escrows for taxes, interest, and insurance. Because you probably paid these amounts at your previous settlement, they will not represent an out-of-pocket expense of refinancing, as your prepayments will be transferred to your new account. However, if new

statutes or ordinances have come into effect since your last
settlement, you may have to lay out some additional cash.

The Grand Total

Your refinancing costs (excluding the cost of an attorney or
other professional you might hire and excluding any prepayment
penalty on your old mortgage) may look something like this:

	Size of Mortgage	
	$100,000	$40,000
General Fees—3 points.............	$3,000	$1,200
Title Insurance (if over 3 years).....	1,000	1,000
[Title Insurance (if under 3 years)]	[500]	[500]
Appraisal.........................	250	250
Miscellaneous	250	250
TOTAL	$4,500–4,000	$2,700–2,200

8

THE 3% SOLUTION

In Chapter 9, we will deal in detail with the problem of offsetting refinancing costs against refinancing benefits. But let us state a rough-and-ready rule which applies in a surprisingly large number of refinancing situations and which we call the 3% solution. This means that, if the *mortgage interest rate* you can obtain is 3% *less* than what you are paying now, *and you plan to stay in your home more than 2 years,* refinancing probably will pay off, assuming refinancing charges of approximately $5,000, and assuming also that your mortgage is sizable enough for the refinancing effort to be worthwhile.

Some experts state that refinancing usually pays off if the interest rate differential is 2% or more. We will only say that if the differential is less than 3%, calculate with extra care. A small differential may take several years to produce net cash savings.

Let's look at some examples. If you have a $100,000, 30-year mortgage at a 13% fixed rate, your monthly payment (excluding taxes and other added charges) is $1106.19. If you refinance this same mortgage at 9½%, your monthly payment will be $840.85, or a savings of $265 per month. If refinancing costs are $5,000, it will take approximately 19 months for you to recoup your out-of-pocket expenses before you begin to net actual savings. If you plan to stay in your house longer than 2 years, refinancing will pay handsomely.

Here's another example. If you currently have a 30-year fixed-rate mortgage loan of $40,000 at 14%, and you can refinance with a 30-year fixed-rate loan at 10%, then, assuming the other costs are not out of line and that you plan to own your home for more than two more years, refinancing with a 4% interest difference will prove a bargain. At 14%, you are paying $473.95 each month. After you refinance at 10%, your monthly payments will be $351.02, for a saving of $122.93. Assuming refinancing costs of $3,200 (based on 3 points and other charges), it will take you 26 months (just over 2 years) to begin actually to save money on the refinancing.

Here's a third example: Assume a 15-year, 13½% fixed-rate mortgage loan of $75,000. Let's say that you can refinance the same amount for 15 years at 10¼%. You were paying $973.73 monthly; after refinancing you will pay $817.46 monthly, a saving of $156.27. Assuming refinancing costs of $4,250 (based on 3 points and other charges), it will take you 27 months (about 2¼ years) to recoup. If you plan to remain in your home for that long, the refinancing makes good sense.

Now let's take a very different situation. Let's say that you have a $70,000, 30-year ARM on which the interest rate started at 13% but has now declined to 10½% because of the decline in interest rates. Let's say that you can obtain a new fixed-rate mortgage at 9½%. Is it worth refinancing? The reduction in your monthly payment will not be great, and it will take a long time for the monthly savings to offset your initial refinancing costs. However, you might consider refinancing as a protective measure in case interest rates begin to climb again in the future, boosting the cost of your ARM. This is a much closer call than many refinancing situations. Here's how the figures might work out:

When your ARM interest was at 13%, you paid $774.33 monthly. Now that your interest is 10½%, you pay $640.31. If you refinance at 9½%, you will pay $588.59 monthly. Assuming refinancing costs of $4,100 (based on 3 points and other charges), it will take you almost seven years actually to realize any cash savings. Nevertheless, if you see a risk of interest rates rising again—and no one can be sure that won't happen—then you may be more secure and comfortable with a fixed-rate mortgage.

9
THE MATHEMATICS OF REFINANCING

This chapter consists mainly of numbers, not words. To show you how refinancing works in typical cases, we have provided 10 tables. The tables are arranged according to the term and interest rate of your old mortgage—either a 15-year or a 30-year term, with interest rates shown in steps from 12% to 16%.

In each case you can see the benefit of refinancing with a new mortgage at from 9% to 11% (in steps of ¼%). The tables show both your monthly saving, and your total interest saving over the life of the loan.

To use the tables, first estimate your cost of refinancing as shown in Chapter 7. Then calculate the number of months it will take for your cash savings to equal the refinancing cost:

$$\text{Number of Months} = \frac{\text{Cost of Refinancing}}{\text{Monthly Saving}}$$

Then what? There's no hard-and-fast rule. If you will recoup the costs in 24 months (2 years) or less, the refinancing should be very attractive. If it will take more than 48 months (4 years), the refinancing is hardly exciting but may still be justified by other benefits, such as the security of switching from an ARM to a fixed-rate mortgage.

If the payoff will take between two and four years, you have to exercise judgment and consider your own individual situation. Can you easily invest extra cash now in refinancing in order to give yourself future benefits? Which approach will make you more comfortable? Remember that if you pass up refinancing opportunities now, it is still possible that you will be lucky and that interest rates will decline further, so that you will have the chance of a more favorable deal later on. Although refinancing is attractive to many people, don't be stampeded into it if it doesn't fit your own situation.

Refinancing 30-year, 12% mortgage loans of various siz

Amt. of Mortgage	Interest Rate on New Mortgage			
	12%	11%	10.75%	10.5
$40,000				
monthly payment	411.44	380.92	373.39	365
monthly saving	—	30.52	38.05	45
interest saving over life of loan	—	10,987	13,698	16,
$70,000				
monthly payment	720.02	666.62	653.43	640
monthly saving	—	53.40	66.59	79
interest saving over life of loan	—	19,224	23,972	28,
$100,000				
monthly payment	1028.61	952.32	933.48	914
monthly saving	—	76.29	95.13	113
interest saving over life of loan	—	27,464	34,247	40,

Refinancing 15-year, 12% mortgage loans of various siz

Amt. of Mortgage	Interest Rate on New Mortgage			
	12%	11%	10.75%	10.5
$40,000				
monthly payment	480.06	454.63	448.37	442
monthly saving	—	25.43	31.69	37
interest saving over life of loan	—	4,577	5,704	6,
$70,000				
monthly payment	840.11	795.61	784.66	773
monthly saving	—	44.50	55.45	66
interest saving over life of loan	—	8,010	9,981	11,
$100,000				
monthly payment	1200.16	1136.59	1120.94	1105
monthly saving	—	63.57	79.22	9
interest saving over life of loan	—	11,443	14,260	17,

Interest Rate on New Mortgage				
10.25%	10%	9.50%	9.25%	9%
358.44	351.02	336.34	329.07	321.84
53.00	60.42	75.10	82.37	89.60
19,080	21,751	27,036	29,653	32,256
627.27	614.30	588.59	575.87	563.23
92.75	105.72	131.43	144.15	156.79
33,390	38,059	47,315	51,894	56,444
896.10	877.57	840.85	822.67	804.62
132.51	151.04	187.76	205.94	223.99
47,704	54,374	67,594	74,138	80,636

Interest Rate on New Mortgage				
10.25%	10%	9.50%	9.25%	9%
435.98	429.84	417.68	411.67	405.70
44.08	50.22	62.38	68.39	74.36
7,934	9,040	11,228	12,308	13,385
762.96	752.22	730.95	720.43	709.98
77.15	87.89	109.16	119.68	130.13
13,887	15,820	19,649	21,542	23,423
1089.95	1074.60	1044.22	1029.19	1014.26
110.21	125.56	155.94	170.97	185.90
19,838	22,601	28,069	30,775	33,462

Refinancing 30-year, 13% mortgage loans of various sizes

Amt. of Mortgage	Interest Rate on New Mortgage			
	13%	11%	10.75%	10.50%
$40,000				
monthly payment	442.47	380.92	373.39	365.8
monthly saving	—	61.55	69.08	76.5
interest saving over life of loan	—	22,158	24,869	27,56
$70,000				
monthly payment	774.33	666.62	653.43	640.3
monthly saving	—	107.71	120.90	134.0
interest saving over life of loan	—	38,776	43,524	48,24
$100,000				
monthly payment	1106.19	952.32	933.48	914.7
monthly saving	—	153.87	172.71	191.4
interest saving over life of loan	—	55,393	62,176	68,92

Refinancing 15-year, 13% mortgage loans of various sizes

Amt. of Mortgage	Interest Rate on New Mortgage			
	13%	11%	10.75%	10.50%
$40,000				
monthly payment	506.09	454.63	448.37	442.1
monthly saving	—	51.46	57.72	63.9
interest saving over life of loan	—	9,263	10,390	11,50
$70,000				
monthly payment	885.66	795.61	784.66	773.7
monthly saving	—	90.05	101.00	111.8
interest saving over life of loan	—	16,209	18,180	20,14
$100,000				
monthly payment	1265.24	1136.59	1120.94	1105.3
monthly saving	—	128.65	144.30	159.8
interest saving over life of loan	—	23,157	25,974	28,77

Interest Rate on New Mortgage				
0.25%	10%	9.50%	9.25%	9%
358.44	351.02	336.34	329.07	321.84
84.03	91.45	106.13	113.40	120.63
30,251	32,922	38,207	40,824	43,427
627.27	614.30	588.59	575.87	563.23
147.06	160.03	185.74	198.46	211.10
52,942	57,611	66,866	71,446	75,996
896.10	877.57	840.85	822.67	804.62
210.09	228.62	265.34	283.52	301.57
75,632	82,303	95,522	102,067	108,565

Interest Rate on New Mortgage				
0.25%	10%	9.50%	9.25%	9%
435.98	429.84	417.68	411.67	405.70
70.11	76.25	88.41	94.42	100.39
12,620	13,725	15,914	16,996	18,070
762.96	752.22	730.95	720.43	709.98
122.70	133.44	154.71	165.23	175.68
22,086	24,019	27,848	29,741	31,622
089.95	1074.60	1044.22	1029.19	1014.26
175.29	190.64	221.02	236.05	250.98
31,552	34,315	39,784	42,489	45,176

Refinancing 30-year, 14% mortgage loans of various sizes

Amt. of Mortgage	Interest Rate on New Mortgage			
	14%	11%	10.75%	10.50%
$40,000				
monthly payment	473.95	380.92	373.39	365.8
monthly saving	—	93.03	100.56	108.0
interest saving over life of loan	—	33,491	36,202	38,90
$70,000				
monthly payment	829.41	666.62	653.43	640.3
monthly saving	—	162.79	175.98	189.1
interest saving over life of loan	—	58,604	63,353	68,07
$100,000				
monthly payment	1184.87	952.32	933.48	914.7
monthly saving	—	232.55	251.39	270.1
interest saving over life of loan	—	83,718	90,500	97,25

Refinancing 15-year, 14% mortgage loans of various sizes

Amt. of Mortgage	Interest Rate on New Mortgage			
	14%	11%	10.75%	10.50%
$40,000				
monthly payment	532.64	454.63	448.37	442.1
monthly saving	—	78.01	84.32	90.5
interest saving over life of loan	—	14,042	15,178	16,29
$70,000				
monthly payment	932.21	795.61	784.66	773.7
monthly saving	—	136.60	147.55	158.4
interest saving over life of loan	—	24,588	26,559	28,51
$100,000				
monthly payment	1331.74	1136.59	1120.94	1105.3
monthly saving	—	195.15	210.80	226.3
interest saving over life of loan	—	35,127	37,944	40,74

Interest Rate on New Mortgage				
10.25%	10%	9.50%	9.25%	9%
358.44	351.02	336.34	329.07	321.84
115.51	122.93	137.61	144.88	152.11
41,584	44,255	49,540	52,157	54,760
627.27	614.30	588.59	575.87	563.23
202.14	215.11	240.82	253.54	266.18
72,770	77,440	86,695	91,274	95,825
896.10	877.57	840.85	822.67	804.62
288.77	307.30	344.02	362.20	380.25
103,957	110,628	123,847	130,392	136,890

Interest Rate on New Mortgage				
10.25%	10%	9.50%	9.25%	9%
435.98	429.84	417.68	411.67	405.70
96.71	102.85	115.01	121.02	126.94
17,408	18,504	20,702	21,784	22,849
762.96	752.22	730.95	720.43	709.98
169.25	179.99	201.26	211.78	222.23
30,465	32,398	36,227	38,120	40,001
1089.95	1074.60	1044.22	1029.19	1014.26
241.79	257.14	287.52	302.55	317.48
43,522	46,285	51,754	54,459	57,146

Refinancing 30-year, 15% mortgage loans of various sizes:

Amt. of Mortgage	Interest Rate on New Mortgage			
	15%	11%	10.75%	10.50%
$40,000				
monthly payment	505.77	380.92	373.39	365.89
monthly saving	—	124.85	132.38	139.88
interest saving over life of loan	—	44,946	47,657	50,357
$70,000				
monthly payment	885.11	662.62	653.43	640.31
monthly saving	—	222.49	231.68	244.80
interest saving over life of loan	—	80,096	83,405	88,128
$100,000				
monthly payment	1264.44	952.32	933.48	914.73
monthly saving	—	312.12	330.96	349.71
interest saving over life of loan	—	112,363	119,146	125,896

Refinancing 15-year, 15% mortgage loans of various sizes:

Amt. of Mortgage	Interest Rate on New Mortgage			
	15%	11%	10.75%	10.50%
$40,000				
monthly payment	559.83	454.63	448.37	442.15
monthly saving	—	105.20	111.46	117.68
interest saving over life of loan	—	18,936	20,063	21,182
$70,000				
monthly payment	979.71	795.61	784.66	773.77
monthly saving	—	184.10	195.05	205.94
interest saving over life of loan	—	33,138	35,109	37,069
$100,000				
monthly payment	1399.58	1136.59	1120.94	1105.39
monthly saving	—	262.99	278.64	294.19
interest saving over life of loan	—	47,338	50,155	52,954

48

Interest Rate on New Mortgage				
0.25%	10%	9.50%	9.25%	9%
358.44	351.02	336.34	329.07	321.84
147.33	154.75	169.43	176.70	183.93
53,039	55,710	60,995	63,612	66,215
627.27	614.30	588.59	575.87	563.23
257.84	270.81	296.52	309.24	321.88
92,822	97,492	106,747	111,326	115,877
896.10	877.57	840.85	822.67	804.62
368.34	386.87	423.59	441.77	459.82
32,602	139,273	152,492	159,037	165,535

Interest Rate on New Mortgage				
0.25%	10%	9.50%	9.25%	9%
435.98	429.84	417.68	411.67	405.70
123.85	129.99	142.15	148.16	154.13
22,293	23,398	25,587	26,669	27,743
762.96	752.22	730.95	720.43	709.98
216.75	227.49	248.76	259.28	269.73
39,015	40,948	44,777	46,670	48,551
089.95	1074.60	1044.22	1029.19	1014.26
309.63	324.98	355.36	370.39	385.32
55,733	58,496	63,965	66,670	69,358

Refinancing 30-year, 16% mortgage loans of various sizes

Amt. of Mortgage	Interest Rate on New Mortgage			
	16%	11%	10.75%	10.50%
$40,000				
monthly payment	537.90	380.92	373.39	365.8
monthly saving	—	156.98	164.51	172.0
interest saving over life of loan	—	56,513	59,224	61,92
$70,000				
monthly payment	941.32	666.62	653.43	640.3
monthly saving	—	274.70	287.89	301.0
interest saving over life of loan	—	98,892	103,640	108,36
$100,000				
monthly payment	1344.75	952.32	933.48	914.7
monthly saving	—	392.43	411.27	430.0
interest saving over life of loan	—	141,275	148,057	154,80

Refinancing 15-year, 16% mortgage loans of various sizes

Amt. of Mortgage	Interest Rate on New Mortgage			
	16%	11%	10.75%	10.50%
$40,000				
monthly payment	587.48	454.63	448.37	442.1
monthly saving	—	132.85	139.11	145.3
interest saving over life of loan	—	23,913	25,040	26,15
$70,000				
monthly payment	1028.09	795.61	784.66	773.7
monthly saving	—	232.48	243.43	254.3
interest saving over life of loan	—	41,846	43,817	45,77
$100,000				
monthly payment	1468.70	1136.59	1120.94	1105.3
monthly saving	—	332.11	347.76	363.3
interest saving over life of loan	—	59,780	62,597	65,39

	Interest Rate on New Mortgage			
0.25%	10%	9.50%	9.25%	9%
358.44	351.02	336.34	329.07	321.84
179.46	186.88	201.56	208.83	216.06
64,606	67,277	72,562	75,179	77,782
627.27	614.30	588.59	575.87	563.23
314.05	327.02	352.73	365.45	378.09
13,058	117,727	126,983	131,562	136,112
896.10	877.57	840.85	822.67	804.62
448.65	467.18	503.90	522.08	540.13
61,514	168,185	181,404	187,949	194,447

	Interest Rate on New Mortgage			
0.25%	10%	9.50%	9.25%	9%
435.98	429.84	417.68	411.67	405.70
151.50	157.64	169.80	175.81	181.78
27,270	28,375	30,564	31,646	32,720
762.96	752.22	730.95	720.43	709.98
265.13	275.87	297.14	307.66	318.11
47,723	49,657	53,485	55,379	57,260
089.95	1074.60	1044.22	1029.19	1014.26
378.75	394.10	424.48	439.51	454.44
68,175	70,938	76,406	79,112	81,799

10
POINTS VS. PERCENTAGES

In shopping for a mortgage either for refinancing or for an initial purchase, one of the choices you must frequently make is whether to pay more money now, up front ("points"), or whether to pay more later in the form of a higher interest rate. What if one lender will charge you 10% and 2 points on a mortgage, while another will give you a rate of 9¾% but will charge 3 points? If a lender tries to attract you by shaving one point off its origination fee, what does the saving amount to if translated into an interest rate?

The figures can be confusing. Your lender can tell you how many more dollars of interest you will pay over the life of a mortgage if the interest rate is raised by ¼ of 1%. But a dollar today is worth more than a dollar 10 or 20 years from now. Because of the time factor, you can't make a direct comparison.

To help you, we've prepared the following table, showing the *approximate* change in interest rate equivalent to a given number of points, for mortgages of different lengths, and taking the time factor into account according to standard interest rate tables. We stress that the figures are approximate and are based on the assumption that the general level of interest rates is around 10%.

Length of Mortgage	Number of Points				
	1	2	3	4	5
5 Years	¼%	½%	¾%	1%	1¼%
10 Years	⅛%	¼%	½%	⅝%	¾%
15 Years	⅛%	¼%	⅜%	½%	⅝%
20 Years	⅛%	¼%	⅜%	½%	⅝%
25 Years	⅛%	¼%	⅜%	½%	½%
30 Years	⅛%	¼%	⅜%	⅜%	½%

One point = an initial charge (origination fee, etc.) equal in dollar amount to 1% of the face value of the mortgage loan.

For example, if a lender tacks 3 points on to a 30-year mortgage, that is equivalent to adding about ⅜% to the interest rate. Or if a lender shaves one point off his charges on a 15-year mortgage, you are saving the equivalent of ⅛% on the mortgage interest rate.

PART 4
THE MECHANICS OF REFINANCING

11
WHERE TO REFINANCE

Where are you likely to get the best refinancing deal? First, check your present mortgage lender. Next, shop around, visiting at least one other lender and perhaps a third and fourth—or more, if necessary.

The reason we advise going to your present lender is simple. The lender knows that if you are determined to refinance, there is no way to keep you from paying off the old mortgage. So the only way for the lender to keep your business is by offering you an attractive refinancing deal. Having already made a profit on your account, your old lender may be more inclined to give you a break, perhaps charging only one point as a general fee rather than the more standard 3 points.

Remember that your original mortgage lender has continued to make money on your mortgage, even if the mortgage has been sold in the secondary market, since the original lender ordinarily continues to service the mortgage by collecting your monthly payments of interest and principal for the life of the loan. By servicing your contract, the lender usually earns about ⅜ of 1% of the total amount of the loan as an annual servicing fee. If you refinance elsewhere, you will pay off your existing mortgage loan and your lender's service contract will terminate. It makes good business sense for your present mortgage lender to want to keep your business by being competitive on your refinancing.

Banking Institutions

What if you need to shop? Banks are, of course, the most obvious sources of money. There are several types of banks involved in the mortgage business. Commercial banks are important mortgage lenders. Savings and loan associations, called building and loan associations in some areas, traditionally put most of their depositors' money into mortgages and are a mainstay of the housing industry. Mutual savings banks (located mainly in New York and New England and similar to savings and loans) are also sources.

Credit Unions

Credit unions may be the cheapest source of mortgage money. Because they are nonprofit organizations, they can offer members many advantages. While many credit unions do not yet offer mortgage loans, the number of those that do is constantly expanding. If you belong to a credit union, be sure to inquire there for refinancing terms.

However, don't go to your credit union unprepared. Be aware of the many varieties of mortgage loans that are generally available before you go. The union may offer only a few varieties and your needs may be better met by a type not offered. It's best to shop around first and know the territory before you commit at a credit union.

Second, check the interest rate offered against other offerings in your area to make sure that it's good. While credit unions will almost certainly save you money on points (origination fees, etc.), they don't necessarily offer the best interest rates.

One important advantage of credit union borrowing is that many will permit you to pay your taxes and insurance premiums directly rather than escrowing 6 months' or a year's worth at settlement. This can greatly reduce the amount of cash you will have to lay out at settlement and will lower your out-of-pocket refinancing costs. Finally, your credit union may permit you to arrange a payroll deduction for your monthly mortgage payments.

Mortgage Service Companies

Mortgage service companies, also known as mortgage brokers or mortgage bankers, are service companies which deal exclusively in the mortgage lending business. They are state licensed and regulated and, because they specialize, they frequently offer loans at discount rates.

58

Mortgage service companies operate in two ways. They may originate mortgage loans, packaging groups of loans for resale; or they may act as representatives of banks, savings and loans, credit unions, and other lenders in processing mortgages.

A mortgage service company will frequently offer you a favorable deal. Mortgages are their business, and they have to remain competitive in order to stay ahead. In addition, the mortgage companies frequently work with the new computerized mortgage networks (see below) and may be able to give you a mortgage commitment in as little as 30 minutes, if you are lucky.

But be sure that you are dealing with a reputable company. Cases are often reported where a mortgage broker promises a mortgage on certain terms and then fails to deliver on its commitment, leaving the borrower stranded and disappointed. It is essential that you know your lender's reputation.

Mortgage Consultant

A mortgage consultant processes your application for subscribing lenders. Theoretically, this allows your application to be viewed by many lenders at once. There is no fee to the buyer for this service, but this obviously means that the consultant is being paid by the lender; so you need to check around to make sure that the deal you are being offered is truly the best available. The reputation of the mortgage consultant is important; as with mortgage brokers, it is important to know with whom you are dealing in order to prevent disappointment, lost time, and possibly lost money.

Computerized Mortgage Network

A computerized mortgage network offers processing plus speed. Your application data is fed into a computer terminal and a refinancing mortgage commitment can sometimes be received in as little as 30 minutes. Once again, we caution you to comparison shop before signing.

Computerized mortgage networks are often located in real estate offices. One such network is Shelternet, operated by the First Boston Capital Group, a mortgage banking subsidiary of the First Boston Corporation. Shelternet locations can be found by dialing their toll-free number, 800-822-5587.

Mortgage Reporting Services

One good source of mortgage information is the mortgage reporting services that are available at bookstores and newsstands in many areas. They tell you where the refinancing mortgage money is, the interest rates being offered, and the qualifications you must meet for each listed lender. They can save you considerable legwork.

To sum up, we would urge you to comparison shop as much as possible before deciding on your refinancing arrangement. The near-uniformity of interest rates that existed many years ago is no more. Don't jump at an offer just because it seems much better than your old mortgage; take time to be sure that you are really getting the best deal.

12
WHAT TYPE OF MORTGAGE LOAN?

A few years ago, when interest rates were constantly climbing, the best advice to a borrower was to try for an ARM with low maximum and minimum caps, caps on interest rates rather than on dollar payments, and infrequent interest rate adjustments based on a stable index. Of course, you (the borrower) took the risk that interest rates would move against you. But in return for your taking the interest rate risk, the lender gave you a lower initial interest rate than you could have gotten on a fixed-rate mortgage. And when interest rates were at 14% or higher, any concession seemed well worth a gamble.

The same advice no longer holds true today, and many of the homeowners who have exactly the type of ARM just described now have good reason to refinance. With an ARM, we repeat, you are speculating on the future course of interest rates. Once rates have declined to a level that seems acceptable and reasonable, why take a chance? Why bother with indices, margins and fluctuating payments? Why gamble that this reasonable rate will continue for the life of your loan?

The answer is obvious. When fixed-rate mortgages are available at reasonable rates, choose a fixed-rate mortgage loan on the best possible terms you can find. Remember that if you refinance your mortgage now at 10%, and rates decline to 6% or 7% a few years from now, you can refinance once more. (But make sure that your new mortgage has a low or zero prepayment penalty.)

As a borrower, you benefit from the accommodative stance that most lenders have taken in the 1985–86 interest rate decline. Given the pinch that lenders experienced in the high inflation–high interest period of 1979–81, one might have expected them to continue to insist on ARMs for protection. But whether because of optimism over interest rates, or simply because of competition, lenders have been quick to offer fixed-rate mortgages at attractive rates. As of the writing of this book (spring 1986), fixed-rate mortgages are readily available. Will the U.S. really avoid a resurgence of inflation and a repetition of 1979–81? No one can be sure, but you have the opportunity to protect yourself now, as a borrower, with a long-term, fixed-rate mortgage.

Truth-in-Lending and the APR

The federal Truth-In-Lending Act requires mortgage lenders to disclose the "annual percentage rate" (APR) charged to the borrower. The APR must be the *effective* rate, that is the *real* rate charged, taking into account all financing charges, including insurance premiums, origination fees, and "points." Your mortgage lender is required by law (Federal Reserve Regulation Z) to disclose to you the finance charges and the effective APR. (Sample Disclosure Statements are in Appendix A.) This can be of great help. Remember that it may be better to pay an additional ¼% over the life of your loan than an extra 3 or 4 points today (especially because the points probably aren't immediately tax-deductible).

The Fannie Mae/Freddie Mac Guidelines

Fannie Mae and Freddie Mac, the two large quasi-governmental agencies that purchase mortgages (see Chapter 5), also are active in the refinancing business. These organizations promulgate regulations regarding the types of mortgages they will purchase. As of the writing of this book, $153,100 was the maximum refinancing mortgage for a single-family, owner-occupied home, that Fannie or Freddie will buy for resale. The amount is higher for multiple-family dwellings.

If your refinancing needs are $153,100 or less, and you meet the other requirements, which are minimal, then you will probably not have great difficulty obtaining a fixed-rate mortgage at the current interest rates.

Refinancing For More Than $153,100

If you need to refinance for more than the Fannie/Freddie

limit, then you may have to consider taking two mortgage loans, rather than one. Mortgage lenders may not offer you a fixed-rate loan for more than the Fannie/Freddie limit of $153,100, because of the problem they will have in reselling your new mortgage. This does not rule out the possibility of finding a lender who will give you a fixed-rate loan of $175,000 or $200,000 at an attractive interest rate, but it does mean that your search will be harder and your chances reduced.

ARM Guidelines

Let's say that you need to refinance for $200,000, but that you can't obtain a fixed-rate mortgage for that amount. However, you are offered a fixed-rate mortgage loan for $153,100, and an ARM for $46,900. When you select your ARM, try to choose one that meets the four *No-Nonsense* ARM Guidelines:

1. The lower the maximum and minimum caps are, the better.
2. A cap on the interest rate (rather than on the dollar amount of payments) will avoid the problem of negative amortization.
3. The less frequently the interest rate is adjusted, the better.
4. The more stable the chosen interest rate index is, and the less subject to fluctuations, the better.

For more information on ARMs, see the No-Nonsense Real Estate Guide, *Understanding Mortgages.*

Discount Mortgages

After telling you why you should select a fixed-rate mortgage loan over an ARM, we are now going to give you the one exception to that rule. This is when you can obtain an ARM carrying a deep discount on the initial rate, compared with a fixed-rate mortgage, and with a reduced *margin* between your interest rate and the applicable interest rate index. (See Chapter 5.)

Many lenders are now offering such reduced margins in order to obtain more business. It had been common for the margin to be as high as 3% over a U.S. Treasury interest rate index. Now, some aggressive lenders are offering margins of 2% or even less and, at the same time, are giving deeply discounted interest rates for the first year.

Don't ignore the *No-Nonsense* Guidelines, above. But if interest on fixed-rate mortgages stays in the 9½% to 10% area, around 9¾%, and you can find an ARM starting at 8% or less, with annual caps of 2% or less, and a lifetime cap in the area of 13%, by all means think about it. Make sure that you understand the effective APR, and the potential if interest rates climb. Compare this mortgage with a fixed-rate one. Do comparisons over the life of the mortgage, assuming different interest rate situations.

If you like stability and dislike uncertainty, you will probably prefer to be safe and choose a fixed-rate mortgage. Most people quite reasonably choose fixed-rate loans even if ARMs are available with an initial rate perhaps 1% lower. However, if you think interest rates will stay low, and if you need a mortgage payment break now, a discounted ARM might be a reasonable choice.

Preemptive Refinancing

Several large mortgage lenders, fearing an erosion of their mortgage business and of the cash flow it provides if too many of their clients refinance elsewhere, are offering a deal called "preemptive refinancing." The lenders are contacting selected good-risk customers, offering to refinance their mortgages for a fee that is sometimes as low as $100. In this scenario the lender offers a new rate that may be ½% to 1¼% higher than prevailing rates being offered in the market, but without the costs of refinancing.

Usually, the amount of your loan remains constant (so you can't take advantage of this arrangement if you want to refinance for an additional amount). There is no settlement, no new appraisal or title fees, and no points. The potential for savings is large, if your interest rate is only ½% or ⅝% above the competitive "market" rate.

If you have a mortgage lender who offers you preemptive refinancing at a reasonable interest rate, it may well be your best available deal. But we urge you to shop around and to see how well you will do over the life of the loan under other possible arrangements. (Use the table on page 52 to see what the dollar savings at the beginning are worth in terms of a higher interest rate over the life of the loan.)

No-Points Mortgage Loan

Some creative lenders are offering a "no-points" mortgage loan. This is a conventional fixed-rate loan which is offered with some of the advantages of a preemptive refinancing, and which may be particularly good for you if you plan to stay in your present home for only a few more years.

The conventional wisdom, you will recall, is that refinancing only begins to pay off if you can shave 3% off your current interest rate, and if you plan to own your home for more than two years. If you think you are likely to change homes within the next two or three years, then you ought to consider a no-points mortgage. With this type of refinancing, the annual interest rate is higher than with ordinary refinancing, but the APR, in your case, may be superior because of the absence of point charges. The saving of the outlay of 2 to 5 points can be considerable when amortized over a short time period.

An interesting note: one point is said to equal an increase of about ⅛ of 1% over the life of a 30-year mortgage loan. (See page 52.) But if you take this same one point over a mortgage loan life of only two years, it becomes equivalent to a difference of ½ of 1%. A dramatic difference!

15 or 30 Years

Should your new mortgage run for 15 years or 30? Shorter term or longer? The answer depends on your own situation and preferences.

Most people, given the choice, take out longer-term mortgages—typically 30 years. The main attraction, of course, is the lower monthly payments. Some people can't afford payments above the minimum. Others see the lower payments as a way of freeing cash for other purposes. The 1982–86 decline in interest rates has created a feeling that it's a good time to borrow, a good time to borrow more rather than less, and a good time to make longer-term commitments.

But if you can afford somewhat higher payments, you should seriously consider a 15-year (or 20-year) mortgage. The increase in payments, compared to a 30-year mortgage, is less than you might suppose. You may get your mortgage at a slightly lower interest rate, and/or be charged fewer points. Your total interest payments over the life of the loan will be sharply lower.

In effect, a 15-year mortgage is a healthy type of forced saving. Your equity in your home builds up much more rapidly. And don't underestimate the pleasure and relief you will feel when the mortgage is finally paid off. A shorter-term mortgage may make particular sense if you time the final payoff to coincide with retirement, or with some other point at which you would like to see your expenses reduced (for example, when a child enters college).

Theoretically, when mortgage rates are low, you might do better by taking out a 30-year mortgage and investing the money you save each month through the lower payments. But would you really invest the difference? Or would it simply be spent? We repeat—if you can afford the higher payments, a 15-year mortgage is an attractive form of forced savings which you should consider carefully.

Payments on a 30-Year vs. a 15-Year Mortgage
(on a $100,000 mortgage)

Term of Mortgage	7%	8%	9%	10%	11%	13%	15%
30-Year Mortgage							
Monthly Payment (a).....	665.31	733.77	804.62	877.57	952.32	1106.19	1264.44
Total Interest Paid (b)	139,512	164,157	189,663	215,925	242,835	298,228	355,198
15-Year Mortgage							
Monthly Payment (a)......	898.83	955.66	1014.26	1074.60	1136.59	1265.24	1399.58
Total Interest Paid (b)	61,789	72,019	82,567	93,428	104,586	127,743	151,924

(a) On fixed-rate mortgage, including principal repayment and interest.
(b) Total interest paid over life of mortgage.

13
APPLYING FOR YOUR NEW MORTGAGE

Once you have decided to refinance and have surveyed the options and lenders available, it's time to apply for the loan.

The mortgage lender will ask many questions. The first request will be for a credit check. This costs between $25 and $50 and you will have to pay for it.

Credit Check

Do you have any doubts about your credit rating? Your local banker can probably give you the name and address of an area credit bureau which you can visit prior to applying for the mortgage and pay for a credit check on yourself. This will give you the opportunity to correct any errors that may appear on the report. It will also alert you to any potential problems in your credit history that have to be explained to a lender. See the No-Nonsense Financial Guide, *How to Use Credit and Credit Cards*.

Be Frank

It's always best to bring up these potential problems yourself and to explain them to a lender before the lender obtains your credit report. By being forthright with the lender, you can establish a feeling of confidence and take the edge off potentially damaging information. Remember that even such items as a recent (favorable) change of job can show up as a negative on a credit report. Be prepared.

You will also have to fill out a form providing complete information regarding your earning ability and potential, and that of your spouse or other wage earner who occupies your home.

A sample mortgage application form is included in Appendix B. Also included are samples of forms used to apply for VA and FHA mortgages.

Remember that lenders cannot discriminate against you because of race, religion, color, or national origin—or, in states that have an Equal Rights Amendment, because of sex.

28%/36%

The lender will compute your net worth, your earning potential, the equity you own in your home, and the amount it believes you can carry in monthly payments. Obviously, if you are refinancing for the same amount and term at a lower interest rate, and you have been paying your mortgage regularly each month, your refinancing will involve a lower monthly payment which, barring any change in your financial circumstances, should present no problem. However, if there has been a change in your economic circumstances, or if you wish to refinance for additional money, the lender's calculations of monthly payments and of your ability to pay could be crucial.

Most refinancing lenders continue to follow the 28/36 rule. The 28% portion of the formula means that your maximum monthly payment for housing cannot be more than 28% of the gross monthly income of all the wage earners in the house. The 36% portion means that the total of *all* monthly debt payments, including the mortgage, cannot be greater than 36% of the gross monthly income of all the wage earners.

Commitment Letters

Once you and the lender have agreed on a refinancing deal, the terms and conditions of your loan will be set down in a letter written by the mortgage lender called a "Commitment Letter."

Make sure that the terms and conditions of the mortgage as set forth in the letter are precisely as you understand them. Ask promptly for clarification of any doubtful areas.

For your convenience, we have included a sample commitment letter in Appendix C.

Locking in an Interest Rate

Usually the lender will not lock in an interest rate until the loan is processed and approved, a procedure that could take 60 or even 90 days. If interest rates are particularly favorable at the time you apply, you should try to find a lender who will commit to the rate then in effect.

You can usually pay a lender to lock in the interest rate at the time of application. This can be well worth doing unless you strongly believe that interest rates are heading down.

Your lender usually will charge you one point (1%) to lock in the interest rate; some lenders charge only ½-point. The amount you pay to lock in the interest rate should not be lost, however, since it should be credited against the points you owe at settlement. Try to make sure that it will be so credited before you make the lock-in arrangement.

If you have locked in the interest rate and rates fall between the time of your commitment letter and settlement, it is up to the discretion of the individual lender whether or not you will get the new, lower rate.

14
MORTGAGE INSURANCE

Many mortgage lenders require private mortgage insurance (PMI) on conventional mortgage loans (those not government insured) if the amount of the mortgage loan exceeds 80% of the appraised value of your home. Private mortgage insurance should not be confused with mortgage *life* insurance, discussed later in this chapter. The purpose of PMI is to guarantee that if you default on the mortgage payments, the lender will get back the full balance of the loan.

The largest writer of mortgage insurance in the U.S. is the Mortgage Guarantee Insurance Company, known as MGIC (pronounced "magic"). This Milwaukee company was founded in 1957 and has, for most of the time since then, dominated the business. But mortgage insurance is also written by many other companies and is sometimes provided by the lender itself.

Mortgage insurance costs have remained rather steady over time, averaging about $5 for every $1,000 of first year coverage.

How PMI Payments Are Made

You can pay for PMI in one of two ways. The first is to pay a lump sum at settlement. The amount charged for a lump sum payoff is regulated by each state and depends on the type and size of mortgage loan you have obtained and the ratio of the loan to the appraised value of your home. The cost generally is quite high, often 2½% to 3½% of the borrowed amount. But a lump sum payoff has the advantage of avoiding all future PMI payments.

The second way is to pay for PMI monthly. This usually means that you will have to pay a flat fee for the first year at settlement and monthly fees thereafter. The flat fee usually amounts to approximately 1% of the mortgage loan. How the remaining PMI payments are prorated depends on state regulation. In some states, PMI is only paid on the unpaid principal balance of the mortgage, a figure which gradually declines. In other states, a level payment is made for the first 3, 5, or 10 years and then a lower payment rate is assessed for the remainder of the loan. Once the ratio of the equity you own in your home to its appraised value exceeds 20% (so that the mortgage balance accounts for less than 80%) you should be able to stop paying PMI.

You may be told that if you pay your PMI upfront, you will be able to deduct it from your taxes because the lender will add it to the loan origination fee. This may be true, and it may not be. Remember that points are usually not immediately tax-deductible in the case of a mortgage obtained for refinancing. Before you decide to prepay because of a potential tax break, we suggest that you consult your accountant or attorney.

Mortgage Life Insurance

Irrespective of whether or not you are required to pay PMI, we suggest that you think favorably about buying mortgage *life* insurance. Mortgage life insurance, which should not be confused with the private mortgage insurance discussed above, guarantees that the mortgage will be paid off if you die. It's a good idea, and many lenders may require you to take out such insurance as part of the financing deal.

Mortgage life insurance is usually a form of *decreasing term* life insurance—the simplest and cheapest life insurance, with no savings element or cash value, and with the coverage decreasing each year to match the remaining principal amount of your mortgage. You may be offered such insurance by the lender, but it usually pays to do some comparison shopping with your insurance agent or with a few life insurance companies.

15
SPECIAL SITUATIONS— REFINANCING CONDOMINIUMS AND CO-OPS

Many people today are buying into shared living situations such as condominiums and co-operatives, because of the easy, maintenance-free lifestyle, the amenities, and the locations they offer. For more information on this subject, see the No-Nonsense Real Estate Guide, *Understanding Condominiums and Co-ops.*

Condominiums

A condominium is a type of shared living where each person owns his or her unit in fee simple—that is, with the same type of complete and total ownership one gets in a house. In addition to owning the individual unit, the buyer also has an ownership share in all the common areas (also known as "common elements"), such as lobby, elevators, parking, recreational facilities, etc. The amount of this share is usually determined according to the ratio of the size of the owner's individual unit compared with the total area of all the units in the development.

Because you actually own your condo unit, and probably already have a mortgage loan, you can refinance just as you would with a single family house. However, with a condo, the entire condominium development must be approved by Fannie Mae and/or Freddie Mac, or else you will probably not be able to get a fixed-rate refinancing loan. (See Chapter 11.) If your development is not Fannie/Freddie approved, you will probably have to refinance with an ARM. This is not a disastrous situation, if you follow the *No-Nonsense* ARM Guidelines on page 63.

Co-operatives

A co-operative is also a shared space, joint living situation, but it differs from a condominium in several ways. In a co-op, you don't actually own the unit you live in. What you own is a number of shares in the co-op corporation, a certain number of shares being allocated to each unit. The corporation owns the entire development—apartments, recreational facilities, elevators, etc., and shareholders occupy individual units under a proprietary lease.

The co-operative corporation usually has a mortgage loan on the entire development. You, as a shareholder, pay a pro rata portion of the mortgage loan each month as part of a monthly fee. This fee includes maintenance and upkeep as well as your share of the co-op's mortgage loan payments.

As for your own unit, since you don't actually own it, the loan you probably obtained to cover your cost of purchase is not a mortgage loan. What you have with a co-op is a personal loan, which in this case works quite similarly to a mortgage. You will probably be able to refinance your co-op loan at a more favorable rate, much as you would refinance a mortgage. However, it is usual for rates on co-op loans to be one or several points higher than the going rate on mortgage loans. This is because there is more uncertainty for the lender, who holds your co-op shares as security rather than an actual property such as a house or condo unit.

Although as co-op loan is technically not a mortgage, *interest on a co-op loan is deductible for income tax purposes under the 1986 tax law with the same limitations as interest on a mortgage.*

In addition, your co-op board probably limits the percentage of the value of your stock which you can finance by borrowing; they will probably not object to your refinancing at a lower rate as long as you do not exceed this percentage.

16
TEN PITFALLS AND THEIR CURES

Pitfall Number 1—Don't be blinded by lower interest rates—make sure that refinancing makes good economic sense.

Do a careful calculation of the costs of refinancing against your expected savings. Don't forget to take into account any prepayment penalty on your old mortgage.

Pitfall Number 2—Watch out for excessive fees.

The number of points and other charges you will have to pay can add up very quickly and, in some cases, can destroy the economic advantage of refinancing. If it will take you more than two years to recoup these charges through lower monthly payments, be especially careful.

Pitfall Number 3—Know the effective annual percentage rate (APR) on your new loan.

The stated interest rate you will pay if you refinance may sound appealing, but the APR will give you a more realistic comparison that takes the refinancing points and charges into account. If you expect to live in your house only a limited number of years, ask your lender to calculate your APR for this limited time period. Remember that refinancing costs money and that you will only profit from it if you stay in your present home long enough for the APR to be significantly below your old mortgage interest rate.

Pitfall Number 4—Beware of prepayment penalties.

Try to avoid prepayment penalties in your new mortgage if at all possible. If your new lender tells you that a prepayment penalty is required in your state, check with other lenders or ask your lawyer for confirmation. As you may have experienced, prepayment penalties can be costly if you sell or refinance.

Pitfall Number 5—Don't fail to lock in a favorable interest rate.

If things are looking good, don't take a chance. Try to lock in your interest rate by paying one point (1% of your loan amount). Try to make sure that this 1% will be credited to you at settlement and will not be lost.

Pitfall Number 6—Beware of mortgage lenders who can't deliver.

Check the fine print on your commitment letter to see how firm the commitment actually is. We have seen letters that allow the lender to get out of the commitment if someone sneezes within 1,500 miles of settlement. Be especially careful when dealing with mortgage brokers. Know the reputation of your lender.

Pitfall Number 7—If you need to refinance for more than $153,100, don't be talked into taking an ARM for the total.

Split your borrowing into a fixed-rate loan for $153,100 and an ARM for the remainder. Don't be caught with all your eggs in an ARM; this could prove costly if history repeats itself.

Pitfall Number 8—Don't refinance for more than you need unless you have a compelling reason to do so.

If you badly need tuition money, or have always needed to expand your kitchen, refinancing for more than your existing mortgage may be the best way to finance the expenditure. If, however, you don't have such a compelling need, be wary of temptation. Remember that the extra amount will have to be repaid and will also cost you extra interest. And remember above all that you are pledging your home as security for repayment.

Pitfall Number 9—Be especially careful of refinancing if you plan to move within 2 years.

See pitfall Number 3, above. However, if you qualify for an assumable mortgage (see Chapter 6), a new mortgage at a lower rate might be a plus factor when you are ready to sell your house.

Pitfall Number 10—Make sure that your mortgage lender and all the other people needed to process your commitment (such as termite inspectors, appraisers, surveyors, title companies) are able to meet the commitment date.

If not, you may end up having your closing postponed many times. Getting to closing promptly may be particularly important if you have not been able to lock in a favorable interest rate. If you are working with an attorney, ask him/her to try to move matters quickly.

17
SETTLEMENT—THE HAPPY ENDING

Settlement, also called closing, is the time when the parties get together and actually execute the deal. The procedure on your refinancing may resemble the original settlement on your home, except that in this case the procedures should be substantially simpler.

At settlement, you will sign your new mortgage loan, receiving a check from your new mortgage lender to pay off your existing mortgage. Your old mortgage lender will deliver a Pay-Off Statement to settlement which states the amount of money needed to pay the mortgage off in full as of the day of settlement. This figure will include all escrows for taxes as well as interest and principal.

Be Prepared

Bring extra checks with you (in case any additional charges or statutory escrows pop up), several pens, and a calculator to check the numbers. Bring all your refinancing documents, including your commitment letter and your old mortgage. Be careful to check the final papers against your preliminary drafts for any discrepancies.

Even though there is less room for things to go wrong now than when you were buying your home, you might want to protect yourself by taking your attorney with you. As we noted, it's a good idea to ask the attorney up-front how much he/she will charge for this service.

Good Faith Estimate

Within three days after application is made for a mortgage loan or refinancing, the lender must supply the borrower with a good faith estimate of settlement charges. This is according to the federal Real Estate Settlement Procedures Act (RESPA). A copy of the standard RESPA disclosure form is reproduced in Appendix D.

The Settlement Sheet

The "settlement sheet" is a document prepared at the settlement of a real estate purchase and/or financing transaction which details all the various charges paid to and by each party to the transaction. The HUD settlement sheet will probably be used, just as it most likely was for your old mortgage. A sample of the HUD settlement sheet is reproduced in Appendix E.

There are often extra costs that might not show up on the good faith estimate, such as advance payment of taxes and utility bills in the case of a home purchase. Some locales require a home buyer to prepay one year of taxes at settlement in addition to the transfer taxes assessed by state and local governments. You have probably paid these at your last settlement, but it's a good idea to check with your lawyer and/or lender to see if the laws or ordinances have changed and if you will have to pay any additional amounts. The first rule regarding settlements is to ask questions in advance in order to avoid any surprises on the actual date.

Deed

The deed is the actual legal document representing your ownership (title) in the property. It was recorded as an official document when you purchased your home. The lien of your original mortgage lender, which was also officially recorded, will now be removed from your deed, and the lien representing your new mortgage loan will replace it.

Check the Documents

Be sure to read every document. You don't want any surprises. Make sure that your attorney also reads every piece of paper—that's what you are paying for. Don't sign anything you do not fully understand. The time to ask questions is *before* you sign. If you want to consult in private with your attorney, feel free to ask for a break and another room or area where you can converse freely and in private.

With adequate preparation, settlement should go smoothly. You should walk away with your mind relieved and your finances greatly improved.

PART 5
ALTERNATIVES TO
REFINANCING

18
SECOND MORTGAGES AND HOME EQUITY LOANS

We have seen that one possible reason for refinancing is to boost the size of your mortgage and take out extra cash. But what if you want to generate extra cash without refinancing?

Refinancing may be pointless if you are still carrying a substantial balance on a pre-1979 mortgage, at an interest rate lower than you could obtain today. Or, if you are not worried about interest rates rising in the future, you may have an ARM that you consider attractive and that you are content to keep.

If your mortgage was for a low percentage of cost in the first place, or if it has been paid down to an amount well below your cost basis, you can borrow an additional amount up to the cost basis and still deduct the interest for tax purposes. See Chapter 3.

In many cases, the fair market value of your home has appreciated to far more than the original cost. You may be able to borrow up to about 80% of this fair market value. In this situation, the interest on the amount borrowed above the cost basis will not be tax-deductible. However, you will generally be borrowing at interest rates considerably lower than other consumer interest rates. (And note the educational-medical exception. See Chapter 3.)

There are two common ways of borrowing additional amounts on your home—a second mortgage or a home equity credit line.

Second Mortgages

A second mortgage is an additional mortgage loan that you take out based on the equity you own in your home. Rather than refinancing, you keep the first mortgage and add another mortgage to it. The second mortgage lender has a lien on your home, just as the first mortgage lender, but the second is "junior" to the first; in case of foreclosure, the second mortgage lender must wait until the primary lender is paid off in full before he or she can collect.

A disadvantage of second mortgages is that interest rates generally are higher than on first mortgages, because of the junior position the second lender must assume. And initial costs are usually the same as for any refinancing. But second mortgages can be a viable method of obtaining needed cash in some circumstances. Most second mortgages are fixed-rate loans, but some lenders also offer variable rate arrangements. (Remember that in a variable rate arrangement, you, the borrower, bear much of the interest rate risk, which may be substantial.)

Home Equity Loans

Another way of borrowing on your equity without refinancing is the home equity loan, which is really a newer and more flexible form of second mortgage.

Home equity loans are the latest and "hottest" way of unlocking the extra credit power in your house. Banks, savings and loans, brokerage firms, mortgage bankers, and finance companies have all jumped on this new bandwagon.

The Cost

Though the advertisements don't stress the fact, setting up this sort of credit arrangement may cost money. In most cases, the lender puts you through a full mortgage check (appraisal, credit check, etc.), and recording, title insurance, points, and other fees may have to be paid, just as on a regular mortgage. However, when the competition for home equity loans is keen, lenders may waive all or some of these charges, so it pays to compare several loan sources.

Varieties of Home Equity Loans

Home equity loans come in three basic varieties. The first is similar to a second mortgage in that a lump sum is borrowed and paid back over a specified period of time with either a fixed or a floating interest rate. The fixed-rate repayment schedule is preferable if the interest rate is reasonable. The floating rate is similar to an ARM (see Chapter 6), and could be troublesome if interest rates rise over the course of re-payment.

The second type is a revolving charge, usually called a home equity line of credit. The line is set up with a certain maximum amount of money available. You can tap into the line whenever you wish, either all at once, or in smaller doses. You pay interest only on the actual amount borrowed, but you pay the charges for setting up the line whether or not you use it. There may or may not be a fixed repayment sched-ule—some lenders permit you to keep a debt balance indefinitely as long as you maintain regular interest payments. More typical is a repayment schedule of 10 years (120 months). Interest rates can either be fixed or floating; again, we stress that a fixed rate is preferable.

A third type of home equity loan is used mainly by profes-sionals who draw compensation from their firms only once or twice a year. This type of loan must be paid back completely by a certain date each year. The "annual clearance" feature of the loan makes it practical only for people with this type of special borrowing need.

How Much Can You Borrow?

The amount you can borrow under the above arrangements is best shown by an example. Let's say that your house is appraised at $120,000, and the lender's practice is to lend up to 80% of the appraised value. In your case that amounts to $96,000. But you still owe a balance of $60,000 on your mortgage. The lender subtracts $60,000 from $96,000 and arrives at $36,000, which is the net amount available for you to borrow. (Of course, if $96,000 is greater than your cost basis, not all the interest you pay will be tax-deductible. See Chapter 3.)

Some Pitfalls

Home equity loans can be useful. But there are a few important warnings. First, make sure you understand all the rules and costs. What will you be charged for the initial appraisal and the other costs of setting up the loan or credit line? Will you have to repeat the whole procedure at the end of five years, or whenever the initial period expires? How will the interest rate be figured? On what schedule will repayments be due?

Second, remember that if you have a floating interest rate—as is true with most equity lines of credit—the interest rate you pay will adjust periodically according to some index, such as the bank's prime loan rate. And ordinarily *there's no cap* on the interest rate you may have to pay. If interest rates generally rise, you may be stuck with higher interest rates whether you can afford them or not. And if you want to repay your loan early, be aware that some equity lines with a fixed repayment schedule carry a pre-payment penalty.

Beware of Borrowing Unwisely

The worst danger of home equity loans is the danger that you may borrow excessively. The thought of being able to obtain extra money so easily is so appealing that many people will undoubtly borrow more than they need, or borrow when they shouldn't be borrowing at all.

Debt should never be entered into casually; and don't enter into a home equity loan, in particular, without remembering that *the lender has a lien on your house.* This isn't just a personal loan—it's the equivalent of a mortgage. So even if the interest rate will be lower than on a personal loan, make sure that you can repay what you borrow before you put your house at risk.

GLOSSARY

Abstract of Title   A record of the title, or history of ownership, of a property.

Adjustable Mortgage Loan (AML)   The term applied to an ARM offered by savings and loan associations. See Adjustable Rate Mortgage.

Adjustable Rate Mortgage (ARM)   A mortgage whose interest rate is periodically adjusted according to an agreed-upon index.

Amortization   The process by which the principal amount of a loan is reduced through periodic repayments.

Appraisal   An expert evaluation of the fair market value of a property.

Appreciation   An increase in the value of a property.

Assumable Mortgage   A mortgage that can be taken over on its original terms by a subsequent buyer of the house. All FHA and VA mortgages are assumable.

Attorney's Opinion of Title   An Abstract of Title.

Attorney's Record Search and Opinion   See Abstract of Title.

Balloon Mortgage   A type of mortgage loan where regular monthly payments are made until the end of a limited period when the remaining balance becomes payable in full.

Buy-Down   A procedure by which the seller of a house or refinancing owner permanently or temporarily reduces the interest rate to be paid on a mortgage by paying "points" to the mortgage lender at closing.

Call Option   The right of a mortgage lender to require that the entire sum due and owing be paid because of the occurrence of a specified event.

Cap   In an Adjustable Rate Mortgage, the limit on how much the monthly payments or interest rate can vary.

Closing   The time when legal title to a property passes from the seller to the buyer, or when refinancing concludes with the paying off of the old mortgage and signing of the new one. (Also termed Settlement.)

Cloud on a Title   See Defect in Title.

Collateral   The security for repayment of a loan. In a mortgage loan, the property is pledged (mortgaged) as security.

Computerized Mortgage Networks   See Chapter 11.

Condominium (Condo)   A form of joint property ownership. Each owner holds full title to his/her specific unit, with common elements jointly owned by all the condo owners.

Conventional Mortgage Loan   Any mortgage loan that does not have government backing.

Co-operative (Co-op)   A form of joint property ownership where the entire development is owned by a co-operative corporation whose shareholders have the right to occupy individual units.

Deed   The piece of paper filed according to law which evidences title (ownership) of a property.

Deed Of Trust   A loan instrument used in some states in lieu of a mortgage.

Defect in Title   A problem with the title to a property which renders the title not marketable.

Elastic Mortgage   A type of mortgage loan where the amount of each mortgage payment remains constant, but the number of payments required varies according to the level of interest rates.

Equity or Owner's Equity   The amount by which the market value of a property exceeds the amount of the mortgage and all other debts, claims, or liens against the property.

Escrow   Money deposited and held by a neutral party in contemplation of a purchase or other transaction.

Farmers Home Administration (FmHA)   A part of the U.S. Department of Agriculture offering mortgage loans to farmers and non-farmers in qualifying rural areas.

Federal Home Loan Mortgage Corporation (Freddie Mac)   A quasi-governmental agency that purchases mortgages from the original mortgage lenders.

Federal Housing Authority (FHA)   A part of the U.S. Department of Housing and Urban Development that offers mortgage loan insurance programs to buyers of qualifying properties.

Federal National Mortgage Association (Fannie Mae)   A quasi-governmental agency, now publicly owned, that purchases mortgages from the original mortgage lenders.

Fee Simple Absolute (Fee)   The best and most complete form of legal ownership, carrying the absolute right to use, sell, or bequeath property in any manner desired.

Foreclosure   The legal remedy used by a mortgage lender to assume ownership of a property when required loan repayments are not made.

Government National Mortgage Association (Ginnie Mae)   A government agency, carrying the full faith and credit of the United States government, that purchases mortgages from the original mortgage lender.

Graduated Payment Mortgage   A type of mortgage loan where the repayments start small and gradually increase.

Growing Equity Mortgage   A type of mortgage loan where, in addition to the usual periodic payments of principal and interest, additional payments are made to reduce the principal more quickly and increase the borrower's equity in the property.

HUD   The U.S. Department of Housing and Urban Development.

Joint Tenants   A form of property ownership between two or more persons with "right of survivorship." All owners can use and enjoy the whole property, and on death the whole property is owned by the survivor(s).

Lien   A legal notice, filed according to law, of the right of a lienholder (such as a mortgage lender) to be paid from the proceeds of the sale of property on which the lien was recorded.

Margin   In an ARM, the spread between the interest rate index and the rate actually charged to the borrower.

Mortgage   The legal document representing a loan of money in return for the pledge of property as collateral for the repayment of the loan with interest.

Mortgage Commitment   The written notice from a mortgage lender that your mortgage application has been approved and that, for a specified time period, the mortgage loan will be available for you to buy a specified property.

Mortgagee   The person or company who receives the mortgage as a pledge for repayment of the loan. The mortgage lender.

Mortgagor   The mortgage borrower who gives the mortgage as a pledge to repay.

Negative Amortization   The process of adding to the principal balance of a loan when current payments do not fully cover the required interest.

Origination Fee   A fee, usually amounting to from one to four points (1% to 4% of the face amount of the mortgage loan), charged by a mortgage lender at the inception of the loan.

Points   Charges levied by the mortgage lender and usually payable at closing. One point represents 1% of the face value of the mortgage loan.

Prepayment Penalty   A charge imposed by a mortgage lender on a borrower who wants to pay off part or all of a mortgage loan in advance of schedule.

Price Level Adjustable Mortgage   A type of mortgage loan where the principal and the payments are adjusted upward periodically for inflation.

Principal   The face amount borrowed in a mortgage loan.

Renegotiable Rate Mortgage   See Rollover Mortgage.

Rollover Mortgage   A mortgage loan which is renegotiated at periodic intervals.

Settlement   See Closing.

Shared Appreciation Mortgage   A mortgage loan where the mortgage lender offers a lower interest rate in exchange for subsequently being paid a part of the market appreciation of the property.

Shared Equity Mortgage   An arrangement where two or more people pay for and share the ownership and tax advantages of a property.

Survey   A legally precise description of a property including the location and size of the land and all buildings thereon.

Tenants by the Entireties   The legal form of ownership of property jointly by husband and wife.

Tenants in Common   A form of property ownership where two or more persons own a property and all can use or enjoy it and each tenant can will, sell, or devise his or her piece as desired (with no right of survivorship).

Title   Legal evidence of ownership of a property.

Title Company   A company which researches titles and usually also insures them against defects.

Title Insurance   Insurance obtained by the buyer of a property to insure against any undiscovered problems regarding the title to the property.

Title Search   An investigation into the history of ownership of a property to check for liens, unpaid claims, restrictions, or problems, to prove that the seller can transfer free and clear ownership.

Variable Rate Mortgage   See Adjustable Rate Mortgage.

Veterans Administration (VA)   A government agency guaranteeing mortgage loans with no downpayment to qualified veterans.

APPENDICES

APPENDIX A

BORROWERS (NAMES AND ADDRESSES):   LENDER: LOAN NO. _____ DATE _____

Property Address _____

(STREET ADDRESS)

_____

(CITY)   (STATE)   (ZIP)

ANNUAL PERCENTAGE RATE	FINANCE CHARGE	Amount Financed	Total of Payments	
The cost of your credit as a yearly rate.	The dollar amount the credit will cost you.	The amount of credit provided to you or on your behalf.	The amount you will have paid after you have made all payments as scheduled.	(e) designates an estimate
_____%	$_____	$_____	$_____	

Your payment schedule will be:

Number of Payments	Amount of Payments	When Payments Are Due

VARIABLE RATE FEATURE:

☐ Not Applicable

☐ Applicable with the following provisions:

– The ANNUAL PERCENTAGE RATE may increase during the term of this transaction relative to the movement of_____

(Index). On any interest rate change date, the interest rate on your loan will adjust to be equal to the then current index value plus _____%.

– The Interest Rate on your loan will not increase more than once every _____ with a maximum Interest Rate increase at one time of _____%. The maximum Interest Rate increase over the life of your loan is _____%.

– Any increase will take the form of (check boxes that apply)

☐ higher payment amounts.

☐ extended payments not to exceed a total term of 40 years.

☐ additions to the principal balance of the loan.

☐ _____

– If your loan were for $_____ at _____% for _____,(term) and the interest rate increased to _____% in _____ (time period)(check boxes that apply)

☐ your regular payments would increase by $_____ .

☐ you would have to make _____ additional payments.

☐ additions to the principal balance of the loan would occur.

☐ _____

PROPERTY INSURANCE: Property Hazard Insurance from an insurer acceptable to Lender is REQUIRED but not available from or through Lender. Borrower(s) have free choice of agent.

CREDIT INSURANCE ELECTION: CREDIT LIFE INSURANCE AND CREDIT DISABILITY INSURANCE are not required to obtain this loan, and will not be provided unless you sign below and agree to pay the additional cost for this insurance. THIS INSURANCE IS NOT IN EFFECT UNTIL YOU APPLY FOR IT, THE INITIAL PREMIUM IS PAID, AND THE INSURANCE COMPANY ISSUES THE POLICY.

Type	Premium	Signature	
Credit Life		I want credit life insurance.	Signature
Credit Disability		I want credit disability insurance.	Signature
Credit Life and Disability		I want credit life and disability insurance.	Signature
I do **not** want any such insurance or information on it.		Signature	

SECURITY: You are giving a security interest in:

☐ the goods or property being purchased

☐ _____

(brief description of other property)

LATE CHARGE: If a payment is late, you will be charged $_____ / _____% of the payment.

PREPAYMENT: If you pay off early, you   ☐ may   ☐ will not   have to pay a penalty.

       ☐ may   ☐ will not   be entitled to a refund of part of the finance charge.

ASSUMPTION: Someone buying your house   ☐ may, subject to conditions,   be allowed to assume the remainder of the mortgage on the original terms.   ☐ may not

See your contract documents for any additional information about nonpayment, default, any required repayment in full before the scheduled date, and prepayment refunds and penalties.

Please acknowledge receipt of the above information by signing below:

I ACKNOWLEDGE RECEIPT OF A COPY OF THE FOREGOING DISCLOSURE STATEMENT WITH ALL BLANKS APPROPRIATELY FILLED ON THE _____ DAY OF _____ , 19_____ .

_____   _____

Borrower or Agent   Co-Borrower or Agent

If mailed: Mailed By _____   Date _____

APPENDIX B—PART I

Federal National Mortgage Association

TRANSMITTAL SUMMARY

IDENTIFICATION

1 LOAN TYPE	2 APPROVAL REQUESTED	3 SUBMISSION TYPE
1 ☐ Conventional - SFPM 3 ☐ VA 2 ☐ Conventional - RRM	1 ☐ Property Only 3 ☐ Credit (Property Previously Approved) 2 ☐ Property and Credit	1 ☐ Prior Approval 3 ☐ Delegated Underwriting 2 ☐ Approval and Purchase

4 SUBMISSION NUMBER	5 PROPERTY ADDRESS			
	(Street Number)	(Street Name)	(Section)	(Unit)

6 CITY	7 STATE	8 ZIP CODE	9 PROJECT TYPE 1 ☐ PUD 3 ☐ DeMinimis PUD 2 ☐ Condo 4 ☐ Subdivision	10 PROJECT NO

11 BORROWER		12 CO-BORROWER	
(Last Name)	(Initials)	(Last Name)	(Initials)

PROPOSED FINANCING

13 MORTGAGE TYPE 1 ☐ First Mortgage 2 ☐	14 MORTGAGE AMOUNT $	15 GUARANTY AMOUNT (VA Only) $	16 UNGUARANTEED PORTION (VA Only) % of Value	17 LOAN/VALUE RATIO	18 INTEREST RATE	19 ORIGINAL TERM (Mos)

PROPERTY

20 NUMBER OF UNITS	21 SALE PRICE $	22 APPRAISED VALUE $	23 REASONABLE VALUE (VA Only) $	24 VALUE $

STABLE MONTHLY INCOME	PROPOSED MONTHLY PAYMENTS

	BORROWER	CO-BORROWER	TOTAL			
25 BASE INCOME	$ _____	$ _____	$ _____	39	FIRST MORTGAGE P&I	$ _____
26 (OTHER)	_____	_____	_____	40	OTHER FINANCING	_____
27 (OTHER)	_____	_____	_____	41	HAZARD INSURANCE	_____
28 TOTAL INCOME	$ _____	$ _____	$ _____	42	TAXES	_____
INCOME RATIOS - SINGLE FAMILY				43	MORTGAGE INSURANCE	_____
29 PAYMENT/INCOME RATIO			_____ %	44	HOME OWNER ASSN. FEES	_____
30 OBLIGATIONS/INCOME RATIO			_____ %	45	OTHER	_____
INCOME RATIOS - 2-4 FAMILY				46	TOTAL PAYMENT	$ _____
31 EFFECTIVE GROSS INCOME			$ _____	47	ALL OTHER MONTHLY PAYMENTS BEYOND 10 MONTHS (Including Applicable Alimony/Child Support)	_____
32 TOTAL OPERATING EXPENSES			(_____)			
33 OPERATING INCOME Subject Property (Line 31 Less Line 32)			$ _____	48	TOTAL ALL MONTHLY PAYMENTS	$ _____
34 25% OF LINE 28			$ _____	49	MONTHLY DEPOSITS TO IMPOUND ACCOUNTS FOR TAXES AND INSURANCE	1 ☐ Yes 2 ☐ No
35 PAYMENT/INCOME RATIO (Use Line 33 Plus Line 34 For Income)			_____ %			
36 33% OF LINE 28			$ _____	50	PROPERTY IS INTENDED TO BE THE PRIMARY RESIDENCE OF BORROWER OR CO-BORROWER	1 ☐ Yes 2 ☐ No
37 OBLIGATIONS/INCOME RATIO (Use Line 33 Plus Line 36 For Income)			_____ %			
38A	38B SATELLITE MORTGAGE ORGANIZATION					

SELLER'S RECOMMENDATION

WE, THE UNDERSIGNED, HAVE UNDERWRITTEN AND RECOMMEND THAT YOU [☐ APPROVE / ☐ PURCHASE] THE SUBMISSION DESCRIBED ABOVE IN ACCORDANCE WITH THE TERMS OF OUR OUTSTANDING FNMA SELLING CONTRACT.

SELLER'S NAME _____

SELLER/SERVICER NUMBER _____

SELLER'S ADDRESS _____

_____

UNDERWRITER SIGNATURE _____

UNDERWRITER NAME _____ NUMBER _____

TITLE _____ DATE _____

APPRAISER NAME _____ NUMBER _____

FOR RESPONSE TO THIS SUBMISSION REFER TO SELLER'S LOAN NUMBER	PERSON TO CALL (If Other Than Underwriter)	SELLER'S TELEPHONE NUMBER

IN ADDITION TO FNMA'S STANDARD DOCUMENTATION REQUIREMENTS, THE FOLLOWING EXHIBITS/COMMENTS ARE BEING FORWARDED IN SUPPORT OF THIS SUBMISSION:

EXHIBITS

A. _____

B. _____

C. _____

,D; _____

UNDERWRITING CONSIDERATIONS

PROPERTY _____

_____

_____

_____

_____

MORTGAGOR APPLICANT(S) _____

_____

_____

_____

DELEGATED UNDERWRITING ONLY: SPECIAL CONDITIONS/REQUIREMENTS SELLER IMPOSED FOR LOAN APPROVAL

_____

_____

_____

_____

_____

UPON REVIEW OF THIS SUBMISSION

FNMA REVIEWER
(SIGNATURE) _____ REVIEWER NUMBER _____ ACTION DATE ___ /___ /___

A COMPLETED APPLICATION WAS RECEIVED BY FNMA ON _____
(DATE)

01☐ THE SUBMISSION HAS BEEN APPROVED.

SUBJECT TO THE FOLLOWING CONDITIONS:

1☐ SELLER MUST INCLUDE WITH DELIVERY APPRAISER'S CERTIFICATION THAT PROPERTY WAS COMPLETED IN ACCORDANCE WITH PLANS AND SPECIFICATIONS AS IDENTIFIED ON APPRAISAL REPORT.

2☐ SELLER MUST INCLUDE WITH DELIVERY ITS CERTIFICATION INDICATING REPAIRS TO THE PROPERTY AS STATED IN THE APPLICATION OR APPRAISAL REPORT HAVE BEEN SATISFACTORILY COMPLETED.

3☐ SELLER MUST INCLUDE WITH DELIVERY EVIDENCE THAT SALE OF BORROWER'S PREVIOUS RESIDENCE HAS BEEN COMPLETED, RESULTING IN NET PROCEEDS OF $_____.

4☐ OTHER: _____

_____

02☐ THE SUBMISSION HAS BEEN RETURNED AT YOUR REQUEST.

☐ THE SUBMISSION HAS BEEN DECLINED FOR THE REASON(S) STATED BELOW

CREDIT

03☐ NO CREDIT FILE

04☐ INSUFFICIENT CREDIT REFERENCES

05☐ INSUFFICIENT CREDIT FILE

06☐ UNABLE TO VERIFY CREDIT REFERENCES

07☐ GARNISHMENT, ATTACHMENT, FORECLOSURE, REPOSSESSION OR SUIT

08☐ INSUFFICIENT INCOME FOR TOTAL OBLIGATIONS

09☐ UNACCEPTABLE PAYMENT RECORD ON PREVIOUS MORTGAGE

10☐ LACK OF CASH RESERVES

11☐ DELINQUENT CREDIT OBLIGATIONS

12☐ BANKRUPTCY

☐ INFORMATION FROM A CONSUMER REPORTING AGENCY

ADDITIONAL COMMENTS: _____

_____

_____

_____

EMPLOYMENT STATUS

19☐ UNABLE TO VERIFY EMPLOYMENT

20☐ LENGTH OF EMPLOYMENT

21☐ INSUFFICIENT STABILITY OF INCOME

INCOME

24☐ INSUFFICIENT INCOME FOR MORTGAGE PAYMENTS

25☐ UNABLE TO VERIFY INCOME

RESIDENCY

28☐ SECONDARY RESIDENCE

PROPERTY

33☐ UNACCEPTABLE PROPERTY

34☐ INSUFFICIENT DATA-PROPERTY

35☐ UNACCEPTABLE APPRAISAL

36☐ UNACCEPTABLE LEASEHOLD ESTATE

OTHER

37☐ INSUFFICIENT FUNDS TO CLOSE THE LOAN

38☐ CREDIT APPLICATION INCOMPLETE

39☐ WE DO NOT GRANT CREDIT TO ANY APPLICANT ON THE TERMS AND CONDITIONS YOU REQUEST

APPENDIX B—PART II

U.S. DEPARTMENT OF HOUSING AND URBAN DEVELOPMENT HOUSING — FEDERAL HOUSING COMMISSIONER **MORTGAGE CREDIT ANALYSIS WORKSHEET**	CASE NUMBER

SECTION I — LOAN DATA

1. NAME OF BORROWER AND CO-BORROWER	2. AMOUNT OF MORTGAGE $	3. CASH DOWN PAYMENT ON PURCHASE PRICE $

SECTION II — BORROWER'S/CO-BORROWER'S PERSONAL AND FINANCIAL STATUS

4. BORROW-ER'S AGE	5. OCCUPATION OF BORROWER	6. NO. OF YRS. AT PRESENT ADDRESS	7. ASSETS AVAILABLE FOR CLOSING	8. CURRENT MONTHLY RENTAL OR OTHER HOUSING EXPENSE

9. IS CO-BORROWER EMPLOYED?	10. CO-BORROWER'S AGE	11. OCCUPATION OF CO-BORROWER	12. NO. OF YEARS AT PRESENT EMPLOYMENT	13. OTHER DEPENDENTS (a) Ages _____ (b) Number _____

SECTION III — ESTIMATED MONTHLY SHELTER EXPENSES (This Property)		14. TERM OF LOAN (Months)	16. SETTLEMENT REQUIREMENTS	
			(a) Existing Debt (Refinancing ONLY)	$
15. (a) Principal and Interest	$		(b) Sale Price (Realty ONLY)	$
(b) FHA Mortgage Insurance Premium	$		(c) Repairs and Improvements	$
(c) Ground Rent (Leasehold ONLY)	$		(d) Closing Costs	$
(d) TOTAL DEBT SERVICE (A + B + C)	$		(e) TOTAL ACQUISITION COST (A + B + C + D)	$
(e) Hazard Insurance	$		(f) Mortgage Amount	$
(f) Taxes, Special Assessments	$		(g) Borrower(s)' Required Investment (E minus F)	$
(g) TOTAL MTG. PAYMENT (D + E + F)	$		(h) Prepayable Expenses	$
(h) Maintenance and Common Expense	$		(i) Non-Realty and Other Items	$
(i) Heat and Utilities	$		(j) TOTAL REQUIREMENTS (G + H + I)	$
(j) TOTAL HSG. EXPENSE (G + H + I)	$		(k) Amount paid ☐ cash ☐ other (explain)	$
(k) Other Recurring Charges (explain)	$		(l) Amt. to be paid ☐ cash ☐ other (explain)	$
(l) TOTAL FIXED PAYMENT (j + k)	$		(m) TOTAL ASSETS AVAILABLE FOR CLOSING	$

(left column labeled FUTURE MONTHLY PAYMENTS)

SECTION IV — MONTHLY EFFECTIVE INCOME		SECTION V — DEBTS AND OBLIGATIONS		
17. Borrower's Base Pay	$	ITEM	✓ Monthly Payment	Unpaid Balance
18. Other Earnings (explain)	$	25. State and Local Income Taxes	$	$
19. Co-Borrower's Base Pay	$	26. Social Security/Retirement		
20. Other Earnings (explain)	$	27.		
21. Income, Real Estate	$	28.		
22. TOTAL MONTHLY EFFECTIVE INCOME	$	29.		
23. Less Federal Tax	$	30.		
24. NET EFFECTIVE INCOME	$	31.		

SECTION VI — BORROWER RATING		32.		
34. Borrower Rating		33. TOTAL	$	$
35. Credit Characteristics		39. FINAL	40. Loan to Value Ratio _____ %	43. ☐ Ratio of Net Effective Income to:
36. Adequacy of Eff. Income		☐ Approve Application		Total Housing Expense _____ %
37. Stability of Eff. Income		☐ Reject Application	41. Total Payment to Rental Value _____ %	Total Fixed Payment _____ %
38. Adequacy of Available Assets			42. Debt Service to Rental Income _____ %	

(SECTION VII - RATIOS)

44. REMARKS (Use reverse, if necessary)	First Time Home Buyer? ☐ Yes ☐ No

45. SIGNATURE OF EXAMINER	46. DATE

RETAIN ORIGINAL IN CASE BINDER, FORWARD COPY TO MANAGEMENT
INFORMATION SYSTEMS DIVISION WITH HUD-92900-8

HUD-92900-WS (5-81)

APPENDIX B—PART III

LOAN ANALYSIS		LOAN NUMBER

SECTION A–LOAN DATA

1 NAME OF BORROWER	2. AMOUNT OF LOAN $	3. CASH DOWN PAYMENT ON PURCHASE PRICE $

SECTION B–BORROWER'S PERSONAL AND FINANCIAL STATUS

4. APPLICANT'S AGE	5. OCCUPATION OF APPLICANT		6. NUMBER OF YEARS AT PRESENT EMPLOYMENT	7. LIQUID ASSETS (Cash, savings, bonds, etc.) $	8. CURRENT MONTHLY RENTAL OR OTHER HOUSING EXPENSE $
9. IS SPOUSE EMPLOYED? ☐ YES ☐ NO	10. SPOUSE'S AGE	11. OCCUPATION OF SPOUSE		12. NUMBER OF YEARS AT PRESENT EMPLOYMENT	13. AGE OF OTHER DEPENDENTS

SECTION C – ESTIMATED MONTHLY SHELTER/EXPENSES (This Property) & SECTION D – DEBTS AND OBLIGATIONS (Itemize and indicate by (✓) which debts considered in Section E, Line 41)

	ITEMS	+ AMOUNT		ITEMS	(✓)	MO. PAYMENT	UNPAID BAL.
14.	TERM OF LOAN YEARS		23.			$	$
15.	MORTGAGE PAYMENT (Principal and Interest) _____ %	$	24.				
16.	REALTY TAXES		25.				
17.	HAZARD INSURANCE		26.				
18.	SPECIAL ASSESSMENTS		27.				
19.	MAINTENANCE		28.				
20.	UTILITIES (Including heat)		29.				
21.	OTHER		30.	JOB RELATED EXPENSE (Child care, etc.)			
22.	TOTAL	$	31.	TOTAL		$	$

SECTION E – MONTHLY INCOME AND DEDUCTIONS

	ITEMS		SPOUSE	BORROWER	TOTAL
32.	GROSS SALARY OR EARNINGS FROM EMPLOYMENT		$	$	$
33.	DEDUCTIONS	FEDERAL INCOME TAX			
34.		STATE INCOME TAX			
35.		RETIREMENT OR SOCIAL SECURITY			
36.		OTHER (Specify)			
37.		TOTAL DEDUCTIONS	$	$	$
38.	NET TAKE-HOME PAY				
39.	PENSION, COMPENSATION OR OTHER NET INCOME (Specify)				
40.	TOTAL (Sum of lines 38 and 39)		$	$	$
41.	LESS THOSE OBLIGATIONS LISTED IN SECTION D WHICH SHOULD BE DEDUCTED FROM INCOME				
42.	TOTAL NET EFFECTIVE INCOME				$
43.	LESS ESTIMATED MONTHLY SHELTER EXPENSE (Line 22)				$
44.	BALANCE AVAILABLE FOR FAMILY SUPPORT				$

45. PAST CREDIT RECORD ☐ SATISFACTORY ☐ UNSATISFACTORY	46. DOES LOAN MEET VA CREDIT STANDARDS? (Give reasons for decision under "Remarks", if necessary, e.g. borderline case) ☐ YES ☐ NO

47. REMARKS (Use reverse, if necessary)

SECTION F – DISPOSITION OF APPLICATION

☐ Recommend that the application be approved since it meets all requirements of Chapter 37, Title 38, U.S. Code and applicable VA Regulations and directives.

☐ Recommend that the application be disapproved for the reasons stated under "Remarks" above.

48. DATE	49. SIGNATURE OF EXAMINER

50. FINAL ACTION ☐ APPROVE APPLICATION ☐ REJECT APPLICATION	51. DATE	52. SIGNATURE AND TITLE OF APPROVING OFFICIAL

VA FORM 26-6393 (1443) AUG 1975   EXISTING STOCK OF VA FORM 26-6393, SEP 1974 WILL BE USED.

APPENDIX C

May 7, 1986

Harold R. Smith
Jane L. Smith
405 Cal Street
Philadelphia, PA   12345

Re: $81,000.00 First Mortgage Loan

Dear Mr. and Mrs. Smith:

We are pleased to advise you that Jefferson Bank ("Lender") hereby approves a first mortgage loan (the "Loan") to HAROLD R. SMITH AND JANE L. SMITH (hereinafter collectively the "Borrower") upon the following terms and conditions:

1. <u>Amount</u>: $81,000.00

2. <u>Purpose</u>: To enable Borrower to acquire the premises situate at The Dorchester, 226 West Rittenhouse Square, Unit #0, Philadelphia, PA (the "Premises").

3. <u>Payment Terms</u>:

a) The Loan will be repayable over a thirty (30) year term in 360 equal and consecutive monthly installments of principal plus accrued interest until the Loan is repaid in full. Interest to be charged for the Loan shall be fixed at the rate of 12.00% per annum for the full term of the Loan.

4. <u>Loan Processing and Commitment Fees</u>:

In consideration of Lender holding itself ready, willing, and able to extend the Loan, and in further consideration of the substantial services which Lender has rendered, Borrower shall pay to Lender a Loan Commitment Fee of $810.00, which has been earned by Lender issuing this commitment letter, and a loan processing fee of $810.00, for the collection and analysis of information preparatory to the issuance of this commitment, payable simultaneously with, and as a condition of, acceptance of this commitment, and which processing fee shall be retained by Lender if Borrower is unwilling or unable to close the Loan. The Loan Commitment Fee shall be due and payable at closing.

JEFFERSON BANK

----

5. <u>Security for Loan</u>:

a) The promissory note in the principal amount of $81,000.00 evidencing the Loan will be secured by a first mortgage in favor of Lender on the Premises.

b) Any other agreement, assignment, mortgage or other document which Lender in its sole discretion deems appropriate to effect or perfect its lien and security interest or to otherwise secure the Loan.

6. <u>Conditions of Lender's Obligation</u>:

Lender's Obligation to extend the Loan to Borrower is subject to Borrower's satisfaction of the following conditions:

a) No later than ten (10) days prior to closing, Borrower must obtain at its expense and submit to Lender two copies of a currently dated title commitment or binder, in form and content, and issued by a title insurance company satisfactory to Lender, covering the Premises, which contain copies of all identified documents referred to therein. The commitment or binder shall stipulate that a title insurance policy, in a form approved by Lender, will be issued to Lender at the time of closing of the Loan which will insure Lender, as the holder of a valid first mortgage lien for the full amount of the mortgage, subject only to such exceptions as Lender may approve.

b) No later than ten (10) days prior to closing, borrower must submit to Lender a current appraisal of the Premises in form and content satisfactory to Lender, prepared by an appraiser satisfactory to Lender, indicating that the Premises has an appraised value at least equal to the purchase price of the Premises.

c) Prior to or at closing, Borrower must deliver to Lender fully paid hazard and liability insurance in at least the full amount of the Loan indicating that Lender has been named as mortgagee or loss payee. Such policies must by in form and content satisfactory to Lender and must provide for thirty (30) days notice of cancellation to Lender.

d) Prior to closing, Borrower shall deliver to Lender a Certificate of Occupancy issued by the local Department of Licenses and Inspections indicating that there exists no code violations on the Premises.

JEFFERSON BANK

----

e) Borrower shall have complied with the terms and conditions of the Agreement of Sale for purchase of the Premises prior to closing.

f) There shall be no material adverse change in the financial condition of Borrower or the condition of the Premises prior to closing.

g) Lender at its sole discretion may impose such additional conditions as it deems necessary or advisable to protect its lien and security interest or to otherwise secure the Loan.

7. Lender's Approval of Documents and Title:

The necessity for, and the form and substance of each and every document evidencing the Loan and the security therefor or incident thereto, the title and evidence thereof and all questions relating to the validity and priority of the security for the Loan and to zoning, easements, encumbrances and restrictions shall be determined by and must be satisfactory to Lender and Lender's counsel.

8. Borrower's Responsibility for Fees and Costs:

Acceptance of this commitment letter shall constitute Borrower's unconditional agreement to pay all fees, expenses, taxes, costs and charges in respect to the Loan, or in any way connected therewith, including but not limited to, title insurance premiums and search fees, survey costs, appraisal costs, recording and filing fees.

9. Assignment by Borrower:

This commitment shall not be assignable by Borrower without the prior written consent of Lender and any attempt at such assignment without such consent shall be void and, at the option of Lender, be deemed a default hereunder.

10. Borrower's Default:

If Borrower fails to fulfill any of its duties or obligations under the requirements, terms or conditions hereinabove set forth, then Lender shall not be obligated to make the Loan.

11. Acceptance of Commitment:

Borrower's acceptance of this commitment shall be indicated by the return of the enclosed copy of this letter executed by all

JEFFERSON BANK

parties noted below, together with the fee stated previously, within 10 days from the date hereof; otherwise this commitment, at Lender's option, shall become null and void. Upon receipt of the executed copy of this letter and paid fee, this commitment letter shall become a binding agreement. Please retain a copy of this commitment letter for your records.

12. <u>Expiration of Commitment:</u>

If the closing of this Loan does not take place within ninety (90) days after the date of Borrower's acceptance of this commitment letter, Lender, at its option, may terminate this commitment and shall have no obligation to make the Loan.

13. <u>Survival:</u>

The obligations of Borrower hereunder shall survive closing.

Very truly yours,

JEFFERSON BANK

By:_____
        President

The undersigned hereby accept and approve this Commitment Letter.

BORROWER:

By:_____
        HAROLD R. SMITH

By:_____
        JANE L. SMITH

Date of Acceptance:_____

APPENDIX D

Colonial Name
_____

Branch Office Address
_____
Telephone Number

GOOD FAITH ESTIMATE OF SETTLEMENT COSTS

APPLICANT(S) _____ DATE _____

PROPERTY ADDRESS _____

SALES PRICE _____ LOAN AMOUNT _____

NOTICE - THIS FORM DOES NOT COVER ALL ITEMS YOU WILL BE REQUIRED TO PAY IN CASH AT
SETTLEMENT, FOR EXAMPLE, DEPOSIT IN ESCROW FOR REAL ESTATE TAXES AND INSURANCE.
YOU MAY WISH TO INQUIRE AS TO THE AMOUNT OF OTHER SUCH ITEMS. YOU MAY BE REQUIRED
TO PAY OTHER ADDITIONAL AMOUNTS AT SETTLEMENT

THIS GOOD FAITH ESTIMATE OF SETTLEMENT COSTS IS MADE PURSUANT TO THE REQUIREMENTS
OF THE REAL ESTATE SETTLEMENT PROCEDURES ACT. THESE FIGURES ARE ONLY ESTIMATES
AND THE ACTUAL CHARGES DUE AT SETTLEMENT MAY BE DIFFERENT.

L. SETTLEMENT CHARGES		
800. ITEMS PAYABLE IN CONNECTION WITH THE LOAN		**AMOUNT**
801. Loan Origination Fee	%	$
802. Loan Discount	%	
803. Appraisal Fee		
804. Credit Report Fee		
805. Lender's Inspection Fee		
806. Mortgage Insurance Application Fee		
807. Assumption Fee		
808. Application Fee		
809. VA Funding Fee		
810. HUD Mortgage Insurance Premium		
811.		
900. ITEMS REQUIRED BY LENDER TO BE PAID IN ADVANCE		
901. Interest from to @ /day		
902. Mortgage Insurance Premium for months to		
1100. TITLE CHARGES		
1101. Settlement or closing fee		
1102. Abstract or Title search		
1103. Title Examination		
1104. Title Insurance Binder		
1105. Document Preparation		
1106. Notary Fees		
1107. Attorney's fees (including above items numbers;)		
1108. Title Insurance (including above items numbers;)		
1109. Lender's Coverage		
1110. Owner's Coverage		
1111. Endorsement(s):		
1112.		
1200. GOVERNMENT RECORDING AND TRANSFER CHARGES		
1201. Recording Fees: Deed $ Mortgage $ Release $		
1202. City/County Tax/Stamps Deed $ Mortgage $		
1203. State Tax/Stamps Deed $ Mortgage $		
1204.		
1300. ADDITIONAL SETTLEMENT CHARGES		
1301. Survey		
1302. Pest Inspection		
1303. Amortization Schedule		
1304.		
1305.		
TOTAL ESTIMATED SETTLEMENT CHARGES		$

I HEREBY ACKNOWLEDGE THAT I HAVE RECEIVED A COPY OF THIS GOOD FAITH ESTIMATE OF
SETTLEMENT COSTS AND A COPY OF THE HUD GUIDE FOR HOME BUYERS "SETTLEMENT COSTS AND
YOU".

_____   _____   _____   _____
APPLICANT'S SIGNATURE   DATE   APPLICANT'S SIGNATURE   DATE

IF MAILED, BY:_____
                                                              _____
                                                               DATE

(G15A)

APPENDIX E

<table>
<tr><td colspan="2">A.</td><td colspan="3">B. TYPE OF LOAN</td></tr>
<tr><td colspan="2" rowspan="2">DISCLOSURE/SETTLEMENT STATEMENT
U.S. DEPARTMENT OF HOUSING AND URBAN DEVELOPMENT - APRIL '75</td><td colspan="3">1. ☐ FHA   2. ☐ FMHA   3. ☐ CONV. UNINS.
4. ☐ VA   5. ☐ CONV. INS.</td></tr>
<tr><td colspan="2">6. FILE NUMBER</td><td>7. LOAN NUMBER</td></tr>
<tr><td colspan="2">If the Truth-in-Lending Act applies to this transaction, a Truth-in-Lending statement is attached as page 3 of this form.</td><td colspan="3">8. MORTG. INS. CASE NO.</td></tr>
</table>

C. NOTE: This form is furnished to you prior to settlement to give you information about your settlement costs, and again after settlement to show the actual costs you have paid. The present copy of the form is:

STATEMENT OF ACTUAL COSTS. Amounts paid to and by the settlement agent are shown. Items marked *"(p.o.c.)"* were paid outside the closing; they are shown here for informational purposes and are not included in totals.

<table>
<tr><td>D. NAME OF BORROWER</td><td>E. SELLER</td><td colspan="2">F. LENDER</td></tr>
<tr><td>

</td><td></td><td colspan="2"></td></tr>
<tr><td>G. PROPERTY LOCATION</td><td>H. SETTLEMENT AGENT</td><td colspan="2">I. DATES</td></tr>
<tr><td></td><td></td><td>LOAN COMMITMENT</td><td>ADVANCE DISCLOSURE</td></tr>
<tr><td></td><td>PLACE OF SETTLEMENT</td><td>SETTLEMENT</td><td>DATE OF PRORATIONS IF DIFFERENT FROM SETTLEMENT</td></tr>
</table>

<table>
<tr><td colspan="2">J. SUMMARY OF BORROWER'S TRANSACTION</td><td colspan="2">K. SUMMARY OF SELLER'S TRANSACTION</td></tr>
<tr><td colspan="2">100. GROSS AMOUNT DUE FROM BORROWER:</td><td colspan="2">400. GROSS AMOUNT DUE TO SELLER:</td></tr>
<tr><td colspan="2"></td><td>401. Contract sales price</td><td></td></tr>
<tr><td>101. Contract sales price</td><td></td><td>402. Personal property</td><td></td></tr>
<tr><td>102. Personal property</td><td></td><td>403.</td><td></td></tr>
<tr><td>103. Settlement charges to borrower
(from line 1400, Section L)</td><td></td><td>404.</td><td></td></tr>
<tr><td>104.</td><td></td><td colspan="2">Adjustments for items paid by seller in advance:</td></tr>
<tr><td>105.</td><td></td><td>405. City/town taxes   to</td><td></td></tr>
<tr><td colspan="2">Adjustments for items paid by seller in advance:</td><td>406.</td><td></td></tr>
<tr><td></td><td></td><td>407.</td><td></td></tr>
<tr><td>106. City/town taxes   to</td><td></td><td>408. Water   to</td><td></td></tr>
<tr><td>107.</td><td></td><td>409. Sewer   to</td><td></td></tr>
<tr><td>108.</td><td></td><td>410.   to</td><td></td></tr>
<tr><td>109. Water   to</td><td></td><td>411.   to</td><td></td></tr>
<tr><td>110. Sewer   to</td><td></td><td colspan="2">420. GROSS AMOUNT DUE TO SELLER</td></tr>
<tr><td>111.   to</td><td></td><td colspan="2">500. REDUCTIONS IN AMOUNT DUE TO SELLER:</td></tr>
<tr><td>112.   to</td><td></td><td>501. Deposit or earnest money received</td><td></td></tr>
<tr><td>120. GROSS AMOUNT DUE FROM BORROWER:</td><td></td><td>502. Payoff of first mortgage loan</td><td></td></tr>
<tr><td colspan="2">200. AMOUNTS PAID BY OR IN BEHALF OF BORROWER:</td><td></td><td></td></tr>
<tr><td>201. Deposit or earnest money</td><td></td><td>503. Payoff of second mortgage loan</td><td></td></tr>
<tr><td>202. Principal amount of new loan(s)</td><td></td><td></td><td></td></tr>
<tr><td>203. Existing loan(s) taken subject to</td><td></td><td>504. Settlement charges to seller
(from line 1400, Section L)</td><td></td></tr>
<tr><td>204.</td><td></td><td></td><td></td></tr>
<tr><td>205.</td><td></td><td>505. Existing loan(s) taken subject to</td><td></td></tr>
<tr><td colspan="2">Credits to borrower for items unpaid by seller:</td><td>506.</td><td></td></tr>
<tr><td>206. City/town taxes   to</td><td></td><td>507.</td><td></td></tr>
<tr><td>207.</td><td></td><td>508</td><td></td></tr>
<tr><td>208.</td><td></td><td>509</td><td></td></tr>
<tr><td>209. Water   to</td><td></td><td></td><td></td></tr>
<tr><td>210. Sewer   to</td><td></td><td></td><td></td></tr>
<tr><td>211.   to</td><td></td><td colspan="2">Credits to buyer for items unpaid by seller:</td></tr>
<tr><td>212.   to</td><td></td><td>510. City/town taxes   to</td><td></td></tr>
<tr><td>220. TOTAL AMOUNTS PAID BY OR IN BEHALF OF BORROWER</td><td></td><td>511.   to</td><td></td></tr>
<tr><td rowspan="2">300. CASH AT SETTLEMENT REQUIRED FROM OR PAYABLE TO BORROWER:</td><td></td><td>512.   to</td><td></td></tr>
<tr><td></td><td>513. Water   to</td><td></td></tr>
<tr><td>301. Gross amount due from borrower
(from line 120)</td><td></td><td>514. Sewer   to</td><td></td></tr>
<tr><td rowspan="2"></td><td rowspan="2"></td><td>515.   to</td><td></td></tr>
<tr><td>520. TOTAL REDUCTIONS IN AMOUNT DUE TO SELLER:</td><td></td></tr>
<tr><td>302. Less amounts paid by or in behalf of borrower
(from line 220)</td><td></td><td>600. CASH TO SELLER FROM SETTLEMENT:</td><td></td></tr>
<tr><td rowspan="2">303. CASH (☐ REQUIRED FROM) OR

(☐ PAYABLE TO) BORROWER:</td><td rowspan="2"></td><td>601. Gross amount due to seller
(from line 420)</td><td></td></tr>
<tr><td>602. Less total reductions in amount due to seller (from line 520)</td><td></td></tr>
<tr><td></td><td></td><td>603. CASH TO SELLER FROM SETTLEMENT</td><td></td></tr>
</table>

L. SETTLEMENT CHARGES

	PAID FROM BORROWER'S FUNDS	PAID FROM SELLER'S FUNDS
700. SALES BROKER'S COMMISSION based on price $ @ %		
701. Total commission paid by seller		
Division of commission as follows:		
702. $ to		
703. $ to		
704.		
800. ITEMS PAYABLE IN CONNECTION WITH LOAN		
801. Loan Origination fee %		
802. Loan Discount %		
803. Appraisal Fee to		
804. Credit Report to		
805. Lender's inspection fee		
806. Mortgage Insurance application fee to		
807. Assumption fee		
808.		
809.		
810.		
811.		
900. ITEMS REQUIRED BY LENDER TO BE PAID IN ADVANCE.		
901. Interest from to @ $ /day		
902. Mortgage insurance premium for mo. to		
903. Hazard insurance premium for yrs. to		
904.		
905.		
1000. RESERVES DEPOSITED WITH LENDER FOR:		
1001. Hazard insurance mo. @ $ /mo.		
1002. Mortgage insurance mo. @ $ /mo.		
1003. City property taxes mo. @ $ /mo.		
1004. County property taxes mo. @ $ /mo.		
1005. Annual assessments mo. @ $ /mo.		
1006. mo. @ $ /mo.		
1007.		
1008.		
1100. TITLE CHARGES:		
1101. Settlement or closing fee to		
1102. Abstract or title search to		
1103. Title examination to		
1104. Title insurance binder to		
1105. Document preparation to		
1106. Notary fees to		
1107. Attorney's Fees to		
(includes above items No.:		
1108. Title insurance to		
(includes above items No.:		
1109. Lender's coverage $		
1110. Owner's coverage $		
1111.		
1112.		
1113.		
1200. GOVERNMENT RECORDING AND TRANSFER CHARGES		
1201. Recording fees: Deed $; Mortgage $ Release $		
1202.		
1203. State tax/stamps: Deed $ to:		
1204.		
1300. ADDITIONAL SETTLEMENT CHARGES		
1301. Survey to		
1302. Pest inspection to		
1303.		
1304.		
1305.		
1400. TOTAL SETTLEMENT CHARGES (entered on lines 103 and 503, Sections J and K)		

NOTE: Under certain circumstances the borrower and seller may be permitted to waive the 12-day period which must normally occur between advance disclosure and settlement. In the event such a waiver is made, copies of the statements of waiver, executed as provided in the regulations of the Department of Housing and Urban Development, shall be attached to and made a part of this form when the form is used as a settlement statement.

	Seller		Purchaser
	Seller		Purchaser
Address		Address	

About the Authors

PHYLLIS C. KAUFMAN, the originator of the *No-Nonsense Guides,* is a Philadelphia attorney and theatrical producer. A graduate of Brandeis University, she was an editor of the law review at Temple University School of Law. She is listed in *Who's Who in American Law, Who's Who of American Women,* and *Foremost Women of the Twentieth Century.*

ARNOLD CORRIGAN, noted financial expert, is the author of *How Your IRA Can Make You a Millionaire* and is a frequent guest on financial talk shows. A senior officer of a large New York investment advisory firm, he holds Bachelor's and Master's degrees in economics from Harvard and has written for *Barron's* and other financial publications.